LANDFALL 243

May 2022

Editor Lynley Edmeades
Reviews Editor Michelle Elvy

Founding Editor Charles Brasch (1909–1973)

Cover: Sione Monū, *Ao' Kakala Mask*, 2022, digital print on smooth cotton rag, 594 x 420mm

Published with the assistance of Creative New Zealand.

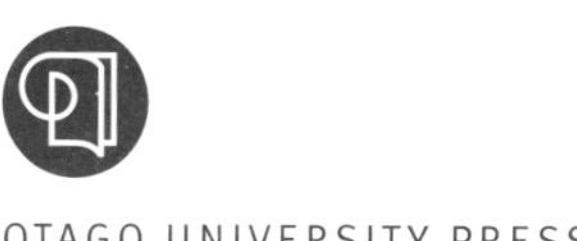

OTAGO UNIVERSITY PRESS

CONTENTS

LYNLEY EDMEADES

Charles Brasch Young Writers' Essay Competition 2022 Judge's Report

This is my first year as judge of the Charles Brasch Young Writers' Essay Competition, and so I went into this year's pile of entries with only assumptions as to what I'd find. To my surprise, there was very little mention of what I assumed would be the obvious culprits: the ongoing climate catastrophe, Covid, the cost of living. Instead, all three of the place-winning essays are meditations on identity. They ask us what it means to be a New Zealander when the concept itself seems so slippery to someone of Dutch descent, for example. They ask how to reconcile one's Catholicism with Rotoman heritage and traditions. And they question how the female identity breaks down under the male gaze. All three essays deal with the question of identity with nuance and delicacy that made them a pleasure to read, and alerted me to questions and angles of inquiry I hadn't considered before. They do what good essays are supposed to do: they take the reader for a walk, so to speak, and point things out along the way: Is this me? Is that me?

Identity in 2022 is a messy concept. On the one hand, we're all encouraged to develop our own identity so as to make ourselves stand out in the neoliberal world of self-marketisation. On the other hand, we're all scrambling to find our 'place,' which means we're constantly searching for those groups and communities to whom we feel we belong. How can we belong when we're so invested on being individuals? Where does one belong in a world so fractured and atomistic? It's not a surprise that the concept of identity—and, by extension, belonging—is occupying the minds of young people today. While there was no direct mention of things like climate change, Covid or the cost of living, these essays, by looking at identity, cannot be divorced from the backdrop in which our identity is calibrated. In a way, to talk about identity in 2022, is to talk about all of these things. I once heard someone say that of all the issues, climate change is really the only one: if we don't have a planet, there's not really any point protesting against mandates or the war in Ukraine.

And yet, we go on, but how can we do that with these issues in mind? To address our identity is, in a sense, another a way of saying how am I to live? Joan Didion's much quoted adage, 'we tell ourselves stories in order to live,' is never really not relevant. We need stories, our own and those around us, because wrapped up in these stories is the question of who we are, where we've come from, and where we might be heading.

Before we figure that last question out (can we ever?), we must start with the first two: who are we and where have we come from. The winning essay, 'Good Catholic' by **Ruby Macomber**, does this with grace and sensitivity. It opens with a short vignette about a young Rotuman woman attaching her head covering in the dark before attending a Holy Saturday service. Inside the Immaculate Heart of Mary Church in suburban Avondale, we hear a young boy speaking to his mother, 'Figalelei o'honi' (Please mama), who is told, 'No son, English. Quiet now.' The essay invites us into this conflicted space, where Catholicism 'took [their] tongues. Pressed virgin whenua to the saturated European sun until Maui no longer felt at home in our bones.' And, like all good essays, its central question—'how does one be both Catholic and Indigenous in the same breath?'—doesn't get resolved. Rather, the essay ends with the author-protagonist returning home after the service to find her brother eating instant noodles and playing a video game. He passes her the game console while he has a smoke and, when it's over, she quietly ruminates: 'To break Perspex, touch tapa and cross simultaneously. To pray with pounamu on skin. What a blessing that would be.' For Macomber, the now is honoured, but it is never divorced from where we've been.

Second place: 'The Deconstruction of Female Identity Beneath the Male Gaze,' by **Shima Jack.**
Third place: 'Liquorice and Ambidexterity,' by **Sophie Rogers.**
Commended: 'The Girl who Lives,' by **Myfanwy Stuart** and 'Searching for Silence at 6.21am,' **Kate Atkinson.**

RUBY MACOMBER

Good Catholic

Forehead, chest, shoulder, shoulder.

Immaculate Heart of Mary Church is my aunt's suburban refuge. The Avondale building may be mistaken for a tiny decommissioned museum. Where weathered tapa waits behind Perspex. Where the smell of incense stains butter between the covers of the Bible. Where someone startles when you enter. Car parks are marked by worn river stones. Anything else would be unholy. *Forehead, chest, shoulder, shoulder.*

The head covering I've used for the past few years is lace-hemmed and makes me want to sneeze. But I pin it to wispy hairs covering my temples. *Pin, prune, prude*—I ignore my cousin's complaints from the hallway about covering cleavage. The quicker the topic subsides, the better for everyone. We are probably running late again.

*

We arrive at 10pm on Holy Saturday. A single exterior lamp provides poor illumination but, regardless, we confirm coverage in aunty's back seat. Feel our necks and knees for skin.

People do not turn around in the Immaculate Heart of Mary. Leonardo DiCaprio could be praying in the pew behind them and they would never know. We watch the bobbing backs of black veils. The hair underneath is maybe light brown, but probably blonde. The other Rotuman family enters the back pew before we do. The mother waves her ili, cooling sticky evening air if only for a moment. Her young son reaches for the ili, but she keeps it out of reach, offering him her hymn book instead.

'Figalelei o'honi,' I hear him whinge to his mama, swinging his legs to kick the pew in front.

'No son, English. Quiet now,' she replies, returning her gaze to Father flashing incense in cassock and cross.

I do not understand Latin. I do not think I ever want to learn. But it's all

Father speaks, and he never speaks to the congregation. But he trusts our bodies know how to pray the Rosary, how to kneel and rise and kneel again. *Forehead, chest, shoulder, shoulder.* The more Father speaks, the less I need to know what something means in order to repeat it: *Blessed art thou among women and blessed is the fruit of thy womb, Jesus.*

⋆

When Catholicism arrived, it took our tongues. It pressed virgin whenua to the saturated European sun until Maui no longer felt at home in our bones. I whakapapa to Te Moana-Nui-a-Kiwa yet pray to the coloniser's God. Grasping for the cross at the end of intergenerational cover-ups, an imposter perched in the back pew. Here my words harm and heal simultaneously.

E Hata Maria, e te matua wahine o te Atua, inoi koe mo matou, mo te hunga hara aianei, a, a te haroa o to matou matenga.

My aunt rises from her kneeled position to approach the altar for communion. Right knee taps the ground. She rises, accepts without question on the tongue a body of bread and blood.

Forehead, chest, shoulder, shoulder. One day our atua will not recognise us. *Forehead, chest, shoulder, shoulder.* Repent and weep whakapapa into awa, watch it flow towards the ocean. *Forehead, chest, shoulder, shoulder.*

⋆

How does one be both Catholic and Indigenous in the same breath? Aunty found Immaculate Heart of Mary when my brothers convinced her to break up with Rotuma for Aotearoa. Boredom drew her closer to the Bible, and to large-print pālagi paperbacks. She spoke of navigating grief by ship, not vaka. Coffee began to taste better than kava. *Forehead, chest, shoulder, shoulder.* She stopped telling her own stories. Over time, *Amene* was replaced with *Amen. Figalelei* and *arohamai* became *excuse me, sorry*. I didn't realise aunty apologised before she spoke until I began to apologise too.

Forehead, chest—Aunty broke her cover when she allowed herself to miss home. Pain refused to cling to empty English. *Mourning like a wave of the ocean, go on unceasingly—he ngaru moana, e kore e mātaki.* My brothers and I listened for our moana, for our histories to break through her throat as her Catholicism was distracted, dampening tissues. Between tears, we heard our tipuna call. Only for a moment and then—*shoulder, shoulder.*

I have a sweatshirt with *Pray* written in rainbow lettering. I wore it most in my first year of uni, when I wasn't living at home but would regularly traverse Karangahape Road with my best friend and his boyfriend. Aunty phoned me for church every Sunday, until she didn't. I would tell her I had to study, even when I didn't. She sees Catholicism in the sweatshirt stitching, and smiles. In her mind, rainbow threads are little more than decorative decisions. Lupe, good, good Catholic girl!

⋆

The road home from Holy Saturday Mass is empty. We drop my cousin off in Māngere and it isn't until we are driving west again, past Onehunga, that I ask aunty, 'Why Catholicism?' Why this *forehead, chest, shoulder, shoulder* truth?

She shows her teeth to the road before explaining to the rear vision mirror that we all need the Lord. 'Lupe, I've forgotten what it's like to love without Him.'

Her life has been a lot of hurting and healing, but not necessarily in that order. It's hard to distinguish oxygen from carbon dioxide when you carry both everywhere. Aunty continues when I don't respond.

'Jeremiah has his love, the—,' clicking her finger for the word in English, '—marijuana.'

She thinks that's all he does.

'Nikau,' she continues, 'has Sara, pretty, pretty girl. He has love. She is Catholic too, you know that?' I wait for her to continue but she turns on the radio instead.

⋆

A while later she swings into my cul-de-sac. It's 2am but she triple-honks goodbye. A bony hand waves through the driver's window as she departs up the street. Weathered tapa wanders to the water, cross in hand, realises the water is Perspex.

The neighbours are screaming at each other again. Distressed sneakers are hung from our powerline by their laces. They swing as if on the feet of the kid from church. Kick the pew. *Quiet now.*

The cross above our front door fell down a few days ago. I don't remember if I took it inside with me. Nobody bothered to fix the hook.

⋆

Jeremiah is boiling water for instant noodles when I enter. He grunts. I remove my head covering. We don't talk. At least I don't think so. But I sink into the sofa to watch the end of his *Among Us* game. Coloured crewmates run rouge in their spaceship, an imposter among them.

My brother wants a smoke, passes me the phone. As the game finishes, the imposter figure floats untethered and exposed. Their grey mask covers any sign of fear. Spaceship no longer in sight. To break Perspex, touch tapa and cross simultaneously. To pray with pounamu on skin. What a blessing that would be.

JACKSON RĀTAPU McCARTHY

Scheherazade

Language is always fail or failing and when I'm with you I don't want to make words any more, just sounds. Except possibly for *Scheherazade*, occasionally; the string of it, the full body of it, the even temperament.

Every cheek is a petal, every flower is a rose and roses and. Enough of the formal, the meter, the iamb. Every foot falls along the shore, every song a verse too long, every humid window flies open and—

Language is a slope to fall off and I am falling off gladly. Goodnight is a fish leaps into the moon, saying every word except *except*. The shrinking universe between our chests; Scheherazade, who made men forget that they were men.

And closer still: The night-lady sway of a thousand letters and ink. The string. The body. The dance. The snake and snake charmer. This is a phallic symbol. A spinning hand. A too bright. A boy smoking in Albert Park and hating it, and hate, and hatred. Every night is a whole day wrapped tight in silk and satin. Every *come* is *Come on, come closer*—

ABIGAIL MARSHALL

Bright Salt

I nest fried crabsticks in my hands. Ava reaches over and peels off their cases, taking the batter and leaving the hot, rubber flesh.

Above us, the chip shop owner plays Channel Three over a crackle-scabbed screen.

An emperor penguin has washed up on Tora Beach, the fourth New Zealand sighting recorded in a century.

Ava scavenges from the newspaper on the floor by my feet. Memorises the TV's technicolour light. Eyes up, she splits an oily husk of a chip with the side of her yellow painted nails. Scrapes out the inside. There is salt along her fingers, littered on my shoes and nestled against the skirting boards of the shop. It gathers in the corners with Chupa Chups wrappers and villages of gravel dust.

We're twins and I'm twenty, so that's how old Ava is.

The broadcast breaks to an ad for electric drills. It's her favourite from the weekday rotation. She grins as the voiceover comes in, and mimics along in her own way: singing the shapes of the sentences without much time for the consonants.

But wait—buy today—there's more—

Behind the counter, the server looks up from where he has been unpacking tins of tomato sauce.

She need anything?

I shake my head. Feel him watching us. My thighs cleaving to the wooden bench as I lean forward, my hands held out as a human plate. Ava is cross-legged on the ground. She rocks to one side on a silent beat and thumps the floor when the news fades back in.

We haven't got dine-in, he says. *There's no more chairs. Sorry.*

The thing about penguins is that when they speak, they do it with a special call their mates and chicks can recognise. It's a two-toned sound, unique from other birds because their voice-box splits in two above the trachea. The sound that comes out shudders. It's dense, mechanical. Like something that's keeping them alive.

A woman in the hospital over the road donated a box of nature documentaries to the family room, so I heard it once as I lay plastered across the beanbags. A group of emperors returned from a fishing hunt and walked straight into a snowstorm. They were white huddles calling into a sea of frosted fathers and babies. In the video, when the families found each other, the ones who had been away opened wide.

Coughed.

Gave up mush into the chicks' mouths.

⋆

With the last of the batter pulled from the crab, Ava stands. She sways on her feet and I dump the meat into the bin. Bits gum to my fingers so I linger in the doorway and try to rub out the clammy scent.

Ava looks past my shoulders to the panel walls of the emergency entrance, littered with grey windows. Points.

Four.

Three, I contradict her. Guess I lie, sometimes.

At four the TV in Mum's room plays reruns of *Friends*. Ava's top episode is the one where Ross throws a fit and says *That sandwich was the only good thing in my life! Someone ate the only good thing going on in my life!*

We make it our joke. Mum's dinner arrives on a plastic tray. She tosses the white pot of fruit salad to me. There is sometimes a triangular box, which buckles even under her fingers. Ava grabs it, grinning. Mum huffs *That sandwich* and she squeaks back *Only good thing in my life!*

No one eats. Ava takes apart the halves, sniffs at the onion cheese centre. Sour milk swelters in the air by afternoon.

⋆

Between frying orders, the man behind the counter sluices the grill with water. Grease and burger crumbs scrape away under stuttering metal. The waste retreats down to a tray, to a bucket—to somewhere else. Ava clambers to her feet.

She points to the place where black liquid is dripping down the side of the stove. I know she is asking him what he's going to do about it.

He gives her a half-smile, and she stares with her mouth open.

When he moves away, she turns to watch what is happening across the road. Orderlies we know laze against the hospital fence, smoking and eating from cloudy Tupperware. They raise their heads when she shouts out, their arms long at their sides.

My sister remembers all the TV ads on smoking, so she recites one to herself under her breath.

Every cigarette—is damaged—Call free—0800.

She learned this one lounging against my mother's green pant legs in the outpatient ward. She didn't watch so much as listen, eyes glazed and murmuring. Mum laughed, in her thick way.

In my mind that laugh comes from a tar eel, flopping at the bottom of her lungs.

The cardigan I'm wearing belongs to her. I dig around for my phone in the deep knitted pockets. The screen rests lake-like, full of quiet. When Mum sent us out, across the road to get an early dinner, she said we'd have to wait. Said it like we were still small children.

My mother has grown young again, she's like a sand bird now. She flattens and camouflages to the papery blue blankets, Ward 6, room for two. In there it's all the rush of wheels. Chirrups. Ads. Ava watching *Dr Who*, singing out *Is there a doctor on board?*

*

To fill in time, I sit on the bench and crush the burnt batter at the bottom of the newspaper. Inky crumbs gather under my nail. Ava's trying to get out the door. Not loudly—the guy behind the counter hasn't noticed. But she's pacing the room, flicking up her eyes when the bell chatters.

People sift in, mutter orders, their hands in pockets. Float out again, eyes down. I fold the paper into the bin to cover the naked crabstick.

Ava has found a laminated poster guide to New Zealand fish stapled up on the wall by the Specials posters. A 2D dory groans under the drag of her stubby fingers. His lips bulge open—as if at the time of photographing he was coming up short for objections. She finds a loose edge of the plastic with her finger and begins to lift it away, slowly, like skin.

She peeks up to see if I've noticed.

I blink as if I haven't.

It's like this: there are moments in the early mornings at home when I wake to the sound of my mother's bedsprings, a ripple of joints clicking into place. I lie still. Door closed. I look out at the sky through the crack of my curtains. Watery sun leaks upwards over a streetlamp and the top of the neighbour's conifer.

Across the hall I hear Ava's bedroom door open against carpet, a shoreline rushing back.

There is the groan of weight on wood as Mum leans over her bed. She will be clearing beached hair from her damp temples. Wiping around her crusted mouth. I listen for the *Good mornings*. All I feel are the waves of one voice against the double-walled hull of my room. The sound breaks, then lulls, on my eardrums.

I hold my breath in case—but Ava says nothing.

I imagine: I am a blue fishing boat at sea. It's the eye of a storm and the sky holds still, a bright expanse of golden, slow-churning light.

I try to go like Jesus on the water, to go to sleep.

What is it they say in the announcements, about that? They have 'passed over peacefully.'

But that's just the middle of a story. There's always stuff, after peace.

*

Outside the shop, the clouds are starting to drip city orange at the edges.

Tora Beach residents are assisting wildlife teams to get a wayward emperor penguin back on its feet. Experts from Wellington Zoo say it may have floated for a year before finding its way to our shores—the TV newscaster recaps her main story on the heels of the Thursday forecast.

Behind the counter, the owner answers a faded black landline. Ice-cold chips spit against the rush of boiling oil. Ava flattens herself up against a handwritten A4 that reads Two4One Mussels.

The dinner rush hits.

Not hungry, Ava notes as she watches the shop guy rip a freezer bag of wedges. They stick together in a lump and he breaks them up with the hard hilt of a knife.

I hate ordering food. Like how some people can't pick up phone calls from unknown numbers, or watch horror movies or eat spice. But I can if I have to. I mean, I've done it lots and lived.

You want something else? I ask her.

Wedges. Her face wrinkles looking at the melting ice chunks on the steel bench. Silver sparks glint along them from where a light beam hits.

She hates wedges. The guy side-eyes me as I order another one-pack: fried sausage, chips for her, and a 355ml can for me.

Hungry ladies today, eh? he chuckles, twisting his small gold earring. There's a flick of ice on his striped tee. It has a patch from a band I don't know the music of.

Wedges, Ava repeats.

Wedges? No worries, my friend! I can do you a swap for the fries, yeah?

I try to smile. *It's fine. Sorry.*

Sure?

Yeah, she doesn't really like them, actually.

Don't like wedges? What kinda thing is that? he says in jovial shock.

She's blank, grimacing at the bench.

Can I get my own can? As I snatch a Sparkling Duet from the fridge, I see her turn away and veer towards the entrance. I let the door clamp shut.

Ava, wait.

The till springs open but the guy keeps his eyes craned up.

You want Lemon and Lime?

⋆

She won't sit. She hangs by the counter and mutters her own language. I text Mum:

> We've eaten more chips than
> a poker player. Let me know
> when the meeting's done, it's
> past four o'clock.

They told Mum three years, but it was only one. On the scan there were white eyes, open, crowded in her chest. Ghost piranhas nibbling in the quiet.

Mum said *I guess that's from pollution then*, and sort of laughed, and I said *What's next?* Then she went in for the next thing and slumped in an easy chair, and the doctor said *Shot of adrenaline* and Ava said *Don't shoot.*

⋆

The day I learned about penguins, Ava fell asleep on the floor. We were drifting in the family room of Ward 6, by kids' toys in felt trays. Pamphlets for Ronald McDonald House Services and *How to Talk About Feelings* dozed in plastic holders on the wall. She was curled up, one arm under her head. I'd tried to get her on the beanbags with me but she didn't like them. I think it was the whine of the polystyrene balls when she sat. There were no blankets so I surrounded her with cushions. Put foam bolsters at her back and added a flat pillow that looked like Dora over the top.

I hunched still to stop the noise and watched the penguins.

The documentary crew were following the journey of an egg.

There was a father perched on ice. By holding his toes off the ground he could nestle a dirty egg against his stomach. There was a tap, tap and crumple of the shell. Bits fell away in tiny specks. The camera zoomed. An ungainly wing trembled out. The father's long beak spined down to poke away wet shards.

A slick head emerged, flopping down onto his tough black feet. But the chick tumbled over and off onto the ice. The herd of birds began to shuffle in. They clucked and called as their companion pried at the hardening fluff and bundled it, desperate wings flickering to a stop, onto his webbed toes.

Antarctica went quiet.

I felt the heavy flick of a switch in the middle of me.

The ward was soft, with Ava shifting her pillows only slightly with her chest. Her brows fixed in a firm wrinkle. The door, which didn't close, let in the peck of the hall lights and pen ticks from the reception desk.

I walked to Mum's room.

The blinds were down, to help her sleep. Maria, the woman in the bed next to her, was out. Off having a test she didn't want.

Routine mammogram, she'd said, *like I haven't already got it. Why the bastards bother, eh? There's nothing to squish down there anyway, I've got that goddamned skinny. I'd be a real Kate Moss if I wasn't so yellow.*

Mum just lay there. Her skin wasn't like that yet, not in the dark. I walked up, a flannel pyjama kid again, and stood by the bedside where the plastic frame hugged the mattress. My fingers brushed the sheet. I leaned forward, and she was so small that there was room, but I couldn't lie down.

⋆

There are no more chips. The TV's playing the sports segment, and Ava says *Nice shot, Roger* at the rugby clips, but keeps one eye across the street.

I'm at the doorway, reading the graffiti names biroed on the frame. When a customer comes up I step aside.

The way Ava moves sometimes is like a riptide. She's at the door before I see her stand.

Four, she says firmly.

I move back to stand in her way, my neck heating in the late sun. Shake my head.

The air between us waits, and we wait for each other. Ava sways. Her face cycles through three expressions, quick. Words trip up against one another's heels inside her mouth. She bites down, twists her hands and simmers.

I'm about to step forward when she unfurls a fist and scrapes her nails down over her eye. A pink scratch blooms.

Stop, I breathe, my ears hot and buzzing in the silence rising from the shop. I stumble at her with my arms out.

She falls around me, onto the street.

Flick.

Just before she tips off the gutter I grab her wrist. She lands one foot into a splash of rotting leaves. A courier honks. Swerves past.

Four, she coughs the words out finally, her voice high and tight, and then air.

We'll text, look, I hold out my phone as proof. *We'll ask Mum.*

The guy smooths his beard as we walk in and sink back on the bench.

She okay? He's got his hand on the landline.

I nod.

⋆

I keep the screen tilted so Ava can see me typing. In the text box of the messages, I begin:

I write out the ad for convertible ladders that's playing—*It's a multi-use essential item.* I say, *The shop's menu has a missing 's' on the seafood list; instead of squid, it says quid rings.*

When I stop, Ava surges up off the seat. I start again.

I explain how someone's thrown their chewing gum onto the ceiling by the counter light. It looks like it used to be mint, but now it's grey and blistered from the heat of the bulb. That the thing with *Friends* is that Ross forgets about Ben when he's not on screen.

I say how the Specials Board has a deal for two: one scoop of chips and 60c extra for aioli. How at the end of the documentary about Antarctica it promised *No animals were harmed.*

That a nurse aide sent the chaplain to see me in the cafeteria.

That when he asked why I couldn't pray, I said it wasn't because of the dying, it was just that there were so many eggs and not enough feet.

I tell her that if she wants to feel what it's like on the street before sundown, when the life floods out from the offices and the streetlights feather a glow into the mist, when the bright eye of the storm begins to spin into airborne salt and the gulls rush up, as the chip shop hisses vinegar smoke and we breathe in and in and in, she should come down.

Come and see for herself.

Ava leans against my shoulder, her eyelashes touching down on her cheeks. She harvests the little pills on the sleeves of Mum's cardigan, where they have gathered at the bulge on the elbow—the place where the bend is beginning to shift. She slips each one inside the pocket of her T-shirt.

I jostle her until she opens wide.

Come on, Ava. You're heavy.

She says nothing.

*

The phone lights up. Mum's texted back paragraphs. The nurse must have helped her.

I have eaten
the jelly
that was on the
dinner tray

And which
was probably raspberry
bring me
something else

A small fish
and a fork
(I hope
Ava's behaving)

Just before the Tora Beach penguin, there was another. Four in a century, two in two years—never tell me the odds. It had been looking for food. Drifted north.

They say it landed on a barren spit of Kāpiti Coast and ate sand instead of snow. The glut in its stomach weighed it down like a doorstop. When someone found it, they pumped out the grit and let it back into the ocean with a tracker.

Three weeks later, the signal was gone.

I wonder sometimes what it did after it was alone at sea, set back in the direction of more water. Whether it still called out in its two-toned voice. If it tried to go home, when they had taken away the only thing in its belly.

VINCENT O'SULLIVAN

Premonition

Once they hear how the spiders are weeping,
strangers begin to touch, to console each other—
not surprise so much as fear running through the suburbs,
neighbours checking the ledges of sheds, the doors
of garages, turning the carpets where house-
spiders homed. It was loss you observed.

Dab your finger where you had seen them,
you taste the tears. Drenched webs sag
tangled rigging. Millions drowning
in days, folded legs drawn up
like the legs of hungry children, the soft-
hearted thinking that. The bodies scooped

in shovels, miniature seething pyres
smoke a street's back yards. The cry leaps
city to city, *a webless world.*
Amazing how badly we take it, craving
comfort as we do. Our waiting for worse to happen,
as it will. The falling stillness. Our unspun lives.

The Boy at the Dump

A boy who lives on a rubbish dump
in Venezuela, a boy of seven or eight,
too busy scavenging to think of school,
grins at the camera, happy, he says,
happy because that day he had found
an untouched orange. He can share it
with his sister. The sun seems a different
colour. Then the clip is over. The dump
is the size of a village, it expands each day.
You hear it moving after dark. It is hundreds
of boys in their dreaming. It is oranges brought home.

As Memory Plays It

We used to say, 'All we have is freedom.'
We had so much to give. Headlands of it.
You could walk or drive for a day, sew east
to west as we used to say at our finest
moments, and you've no idea—we had
scarcely begun to define it.

Then we said to each other, we have only
this, finally, to gift one to the other.
Quite without Blake quotations, without
talk of the goddess who was then the rage,
we summoned the four quarters of the compass
to box us in: we packaged each other
our entire freedom, found ourselves in a garden
so close we touched its rose-raddled walls.
In the evening, read by braille of vanished plains.

EMMA NEALE

Porky

My first lie: the time I told my grandmother that rare treat, a school lunch order, had never arrived. A *porky* indeed, for mine was pure greed: I thought Gran wouldn't feed me her cloud-puff scones if she knew I'd scoffed the entire crispy golden fish and chip feast. But my tale trapped her in the trouble of embarrassment.

She phoned the school to complain. 'You must be mistaken,' the secretary laughed. She had seen me clutch the steamy, white, paper-swathed bundle, unwrap it like I'd won pass the parcel, and devour every last morsel. I licked all my fingers, pink-tip by pink-tip. Under lunchtime sun their oily salt shone glossy as glass seed-beads on a princess dress.

Does your mouth water, too, even now, with words like *secret*, *full*, *wanted*, *happy*? But moments after I recall those chips, and my new labels—*greedy*, *piggy*, *fibber*—I realise my first memory of a lie is a lie.

Reaching back to years before, I remember how in a quiet house, my mother heard the baby cry out from deep sleep inside the crib.

I stood by the cot, *denial* and *contrite* struggling inside me like demon and angel too colossal to hold inside my skin. My mother—my Good Witch Glinda—asked calmly, 'What happened?'

I looked to the air, looked behind us, looked between the bars of the cot.

'A ghost hit her,' I answered.

The punishment swiftly smote me: 'I don't believe you, Emma.'

Inside me, iron-dark sand slumped. My bones withered and split. My skin sucked to them like damp linen. My mouth limped, a naked sprat fished up from the living river, its mute tongue spotted with scales shed from a devil's tail.

My name itself paled into phantom, ghoul, shameful synonym for *stranger*.

I felt my presence thin and thin, as the dear, chubby baby was lifted into our mother's arms.

MURRAY EDMOND

RSA

She used to come in every Friday. And stare. Just stare. I took to standing back. And calling out the orders louder—Ham! Chicken roll! Goulash!—from the back of the kitchen, then running forward, dumping the plate on the stainless-steel bench and running back as fast as I could.

Fred said, 'What's biting your balls?' Prick. I asked him if I could swap days and have Fridays off. 'You nuts? It's our biggest day!' Prick. 'I can't get any proper workers any more, 'cept you, you dumb bastard.' He was trying to be nice to me. Prick. Fred struggles with his emotions. It's on account of being so fat he has to sit down to cook.

The kitchen's okay. I don't mind the kitchen, even with Fred in it. I hate that stuff up front. Everyone stares. It's probably the scar. You can sort of see that they're staring by not staring, if you know what I mean. And they've probably noticed me with a funny little smile on my face. Probably think I'm friendly or something. They know Fred's not friendly. There's all these old guns hanging on the walls beside the Queen and the Māori warriors and why I'm smiling is because I'm thinking about me taking one of those old .303s and blasting a whacking great culvert in their skulls while they're slopping up their trifle and pink-striped ice-cream and the frigging canned peaches. Also, the scar makes me look like I'm smiling when I'm not.

Excuse my Swahili but it's important not to struggle with your emotions which is why I've been clean now for twenty years working with Fred, but that doesn't answer why she was the worst of the starers. It wasn't just the scar. And anyway, it's faded no matter how you look at it. The thing is you wonder if it's someone who's connected to something you don't remember from the past. Because I don't remember that much from those times. The worst one, yes of course, because I had to go over and over that with the lawyer so it's stuck now in my brain. But that's nothing to do with her. She looked like she was about seventy-five years old, thin, grey, green, purple, like a little feather floating in the stratosphere. Staring. Nothing to do with me. But it freaked me. People should just get on with it and stop making stuff up. That's what I've done.

So, it was in the carpark. Takes ages to clean up on Friday afternoon, then I get two hours off but I've got to come back and run the whole shebang in the evening cos Fred has to go home and watch his porno movies. The weekly wank. I ask you. I was taking my apron off beside the Honda when I heard, 'Can I ask you something?' It was her. Waving a kind of cloth bag. Her teeth weren't all there which is something I hadn't noticed before. I just wanted to get in the car and drive away, but I'm not like that. 'You see, you remind me of someone,' she said. 'I know,' I said. 'George Clooney, it happens all the time.' I was trying to be friendly but she didn't know who George Clooney was.

'Something happened to me a long time ago,' she said. I almost said, 'Me too,' but I didn't because I could see that she wasn't quite following what she was trying to say. Nor was I for that matter. 'I think you might be my son,' she said. I'm sorry I laughed. I really am. She had this idea that I was the right age even if she didn't know what age I was and that would have made me one of the last eggs in her body, ha ha. And then there was the scar. It was in the right place and all that. And the way it had faded would be just about right, she thought. I was looking all around the carpark, which was pretty empty now, and I spotted Fred shuffling out the back door. I waved and he gave me the fingers. So I told her, 'No, I got the scar in a big fight when I was a teenager after I got out of the boys' home, so, nah, it couldn't be that.' That wasn't strictly true, because I did have the scar from when I was very young and of course that was how I got identified and they caught me. But she didn't need to know that.

Her face looked disappointed. But also kind of relieved. I've noticed that—how those two things often go together. That's what Fred can't sort out for himself. His disappointment could be a relief, if only he'd stop struggling with his emotions. 'Sorry, I've got to shoot through,' I said to her. 'Nice to meet you.' I wanted to say 'Mum' but I didn't because I've learned that cheek doesn't get you anywhere.

The thing is that she doesn't come in any more on Fridays, but I can't help thinking that if she did, she wouldn't be staring, and that would be a lot better for me going up to the counter with the hams and chickens and stuff. Maybe she died. Just like that. People do. More amazing is that Fred hasn't karked it yet. I said to him just yesterday, 'Why aren't you dead, you prick?' 'Wanking keeps you healthy,' he said. 'You should try it.'

If she was there but not staring, then that would be better, if it was like that. It's kind of disappointing that she isn't there any more, even if she is dead. Say she just walked in? Might sort of be a relief. Not that I'm looking out for her.

LOUISE WALLACE

cleanup

in the black, back parts of your mind are big achy lists padded with housework; the outline of dirt, stains and subconscious pressure. the complex mothers resist this. they separate it out using their hard jaded eyes. the only nests are in their mouths.

/

options are offered as though there is a choice, but even these will soon disappear. there is a genuine tinge before your selves separate. each hour becomes fused to the next. you may look calm but that's just a sign of infancy.

/

when it comes, you imagine a frenzied sticky shift; having to suck it up atop a sheet; getting it all out in clumsy positions. but honestly, don't fret; chores simply delay decay. no one cares how long you mop the bathroom for. a watery storm is on its way.

pep talk for a sap

fuck your early education about bras, you've done your difficulties. it's time to get your veins to work. nurture yourself into a normal state. your body is refocusing, it's a test. liquor simply leaves the burden to someone else. plus it's not allowed, dummy. you are just a common baby. and you are about to be thrown into the fire, bigtime. this is about taking your heart with you, taking a rolling break. holidays aren't a thing you're going to experience any more. your head hasn't grown on any significant scale; stop panicking. a pelvis needs to be taken seriously, and you're never going to feel as if you know what you are doing. most days end with doubts gushing from your nose. needing to be towelled down. all of your reason is now held in your nipples. and inaccessible. if you had any interest in law, you would have demonstrated that by now. you won't be expanding your education in classes over summer, forget it. instead you're gnawing as though contagious. and that's fine. no one's watching, even if you'd like to think they are. why don't you focus on how you want to be with the ones you truly love? right now, you're unnaturally quiet. you are mentally counting your no-employment (it's forever by the way). forget it. verses won't help. for fuck's sake, use this time for good! appeal for the use of less plastic. rewire the world against the rich. it's no time to be courteous in your state. get immoral. reflect on some genuine questions for once. *can somebody please find my youth?* no, because it's gone. so get on with it.

KEITH NUNES

Penny Arcade

Walking the dog and watering the garden and listening to Dad say 'Help me die!' and picking up a drink after nine years' sobriety and emptying the bank account and losing it all on machines that sound like 'Penny Arcade' sung by Roy Orbison on the radio in the mornings when I woke up as a kid and Mum and Dad were getting ready for work and Dad saying 'Get up, you're going to be late for school, these are the best days of your life, make use of them,' and me thinking, I just want to grow up and be like Dad who goes off to do important work and makes money, and drives a car, and has a wife who loves him, me and my dad, collecting pills for his *big send-off*

LATIKA VASIL

Another Year

I'm optimistic, although I have no reason to be.

'It's just a mood. It'll go in time,' says my flatmate, Lily. Lily is right. The mood won't stick.

It's 31 December, and the year has been a dumpster fire. I tell Lily a joke I saw online.

'What is eleven times worse than a dumpster fire?'

'What?' she asks.

'Eleven dumpster fires.'

She doesn't laugh.

We have polished off a bottle of cheap red wine and are now moving on to an expensive bottle of French bubbly that Lily's dad got her for her birthday a few months ago. We'd saved it for New Year's Eve. Cheap red wine and champagne is a horrible mix and I know that good parts of tomorrow will be spent heaving over the toilet bowl, but I don't care. Tomorrow is another day. Another year, in fact.

'List the worst things that have happened this year,' Lily says. She is all breathless and excited. Lily's year has gone well, so her love of all things dark and miserable will have to be satisfied vicariously through family and friends. She also watches an excessive amount of true crime TV. Last night we watched something on YouTube about a man in Colorado who murdered his pregnant wife and two daughters. Even Lily found this a bit much. She prefers random murders to family psychodramas. There's just something about the senselessness of 'wrong place, wrong time' tragedies that are so intriguing and appealing, she says. I know there is something profoundly revealing in this little insight into Lily's psyche, but I'm too drunk to pinpoint what it is.

'List. Top 5. Come on,' Lily says. She has her notebook and pen at the ready.

We have become obsessed with lists. A quick flick through the notebook would reveal lists from the downright prosaic (Top 5 places to get Nashville-style hot chicken—another recent obsession) to the deep (Top 5 ways our generation has been screwed over by our parents' and grandparents' generations). Lily and I have decided we are completely doomed: born at the beginning of the end of the world. It feels like standing on a cliff edge with one foot hovering on thin air and the other on crumbling ground. This is no exaggeration of how we feel. Lily is a biologist—a bona-fide, lab-coat-wearing, microscope-using scientist—and not prone to hyperbole.

'I have to think. It's been an unusually strange year,' I say. I wonder if this is the best way to spend the evening and, more importantly, whether hanging out with Lily is good for my mental health, but as she is pretty much my only friend, I guess I don't have much choice. The alternative would be to spend New Year's Eve on my own and I have done that plenty of times with bad consequences.

Last year, for example.

Lily had gone to Hong Kong to stay with her sister for the Christmas holidays. At first I had enjoyed having the place to myself. Lily can be very exacting about rules and routines. She insists on following every healthy eating fad from kombucha to overnight oats—this was before our fried chicken obsession, of course. It felt satisfying having an empty fridge and a kitchen benchtop piled high with grease-stained takeaway containers and knowing that Lily would be appalled. I wasn't a pig, but a little mess and disorder from time to time did one good. I was fine until New Year's Eve, and then my mood fell off a cliff. I tried to trick myself by ordering in a nice dinner of gochujang chicken and rice cakes and two bottles of bubbly. 'Party for one,' the delivery guy had said in an upbeat tone, but I picked up a hint of a sneer. He couldn't fool me.

The dinner was nice. The bubbly even better. I was into my second bottle when I got it into my head that I needed to go for a run. It seemed like a brilliant idea. I kitted up, selecting each item of clothing as carefully as if I was getting dolled up for a night on the town. Layers of activewear were strewn over my bed. I eventually settled on a black Nike tracksuit. The jacket and pants both sported a fluorescent swoosh. I looked at myself in the mirror. My eyes looked strange but I liked the outfit—the swooshes were reassuringly positive. Two ticks for me. Finally, I laced up my black and white Nike running shoes. Lily would have said the outfit was too matchy-matchy but I liked it. I looked like a cat burglar.

I ran down the hill towards Aro Street. The air was cold—especially for December, which is supposed to be a summer month but hardly ever is any more. No one was out running at 11pm on New Year's Eve but there were plenty of people around. I ran through the park and saw a large group congregated around a picnic table. They were drinking beer from bottles and dipping into a communal pile of fish and chips, spread out on paper on the table. I caught the familiar greasy smell as I flew past. I had sat at this same picnic table eating fish and chips with Richie last summer, before he'd dumped me. *Richie, my ex.* He was the only adult I knew who, having been born Richard, decided to call himself Richie. It didn't suit him—there was nothing Richie or remotely childlike about him.

Almost a whole year later I could think of him and say his name without a blinding urge to throw something large and fragile against the wall. After the break-up, Lily had talked me down several times when I'd threatened to ring him up and yell down the phone or, worse, cry—usually late at night after we'd had a few glasses of wine. 'Forget him. He's not worth it. It's a cliché but the best revenge is to live well,' she'd say.

This was true but the problem was that the advice appeared to be working for Richie, not me. He was the one who had effortlessly moved on, buying a brand-new townhouse in the city and, soon after, moving in his new girlfriend. He was living well and I was ... I was running through the streets on my own on New Year's Eve.

I was running at a pace now and had worked up a sweat. I unzipped my hoodie to let in some air. I was on autopilot, navigating the streets based on a tricksy internal GPS, which must be how I ended up outside Richie's new townhouse. He'd never invited me over but I had seen it from the outside plenty of times. The house was dark and Richie's Leaf was not in the carport. Of course—it was New Year's Eve so Richie and his girlfriend were out on the town or at a party.

I noticed a window was slightly open. I was sure I could squeeze through in my cat burglar outfit. I could and I would. Who leaves a window open? That's inviting a break-in. Richie was lucky it was only me breaking and entering and I meant no harm. He was the type of person who didn't bother to think about security. Nothing terrible had ever happened to him and he didn't have the imagination to think something might. Maybe he felt impervious to life's misfortunes. I slithered through the tight gap, in the process knocking over a vase on the windowsill. It was sturdy Japanese pottery and didn't break when it landed on the carpet, but it did leave a small wet patch. I shoved the two pink peonies back into the vase and repositioned it on the sill.

It wasn't too dark inside—the gossamer-sheer designer curtains let in plenty of street light. Still, I used the torch on my phone to scan the room. It was nice in a minimalist Marie Kondo way. Lily would have liked it. I preferred more clutter, more personality. Everything was in order, in its proper place. There were no old boxes of takeout on the dining table, no clothes thrown on the backs of chairs or piles of books and magazines on the floor.

I suddenly felt tired. My champagne high was wearing off. I sat down on a bar stool at the shiny granite kitchen island, which was vast and, like the rest of the place, spotless. It was obvious no one ever cooked in this kitchen. I noticed a packet of cigarettes and a lighter next to a potted orchid. A graphic image of dissected blackened lungs covered the front of the cigarette packet. It was good to see something ugly and tacky amid all this perfection. I hadn't smoked for years but I lit up. I took small puffs, swirling the smoke around my mouth but not inhaling.

I thought I heard a car pulling up outside so I headed towards the window. As I stood looking out, my cigarette brushed against the curtains. I pushed the tip into the fabric and held it there for a moment, wondering how long it would take for the floaty silky fabric to catch alight. It would be so easy ... but I moved the cigarette away. It had left a small perfect round hole. There was nothing to see outside. There was nothing to see inside either. A wave of disappointment washed over me.

I was heading towards the door to leave when I heard loud popping and fizzing sounds. The room lit up intermittently. It was midnight and the fireworks at the waterfront were going off. I don't know why, but I decided I needed to take a souvenir—maybe a New Year's Eve present to myself. I walked over to the oak bookcase that covered the entire back wall of the living room, upon which Richie and his girlfriend had placed a few carefully curated ornaments among the art books and photo frames.

I picked up the first object that caught my eye, which was the model Concorde I had bought Richie a few years ago. I had found it in the Opportunity for Animals thrift shop in Newtown, still in its original packaging. Richie had been over the moon. He loved planes and it had been his childhood dream to fly in the Concorde. He was gutted when it was retired in 2003. He was only ten years old and already one of his dreams had been crushed.

*

Lily taunts me back to the game. 'Come on. You're not playing. You're no fun tonight,' she says. She's frustrated that she hasn't managed to coax me into listing the worst things that had happened to me during the year. It is a tiresome game, and I know it will circle back to Richie and the breaking and entering 'incident'. Lily loves talking about the incident. She finds it hilarious, and I suppose I can see that. If it weren't me living with the blowback, I would find it funny too.

The problem, I found out later, was that Richie *did* care about security and had installed surveillance cameras throughout his townhouse. I had been filmed. He didn't press charges but it was embarrassing, and I lost a lot of friends. Mostly people thought I had lost my marbles and stayed away. I was labelled a mad stalker. Lily stuck by me.

'Sorry, not playing. I'm feeling too optimistic, and I refuse to bring myself down for your benefit,' I say, throwing a small Hello Kitty cushion at her. Our flat is full of *kawaii*.

'Okay, but your optimism won't last. I give it until midnight,' she says.

I look at the clock. Eleven fifty-nine.

I switch on the TV for the tail-end of the countdown. Five, four, three, two, one ...

'Happy New Year, Lil.'

'Happy New Year, doll.'

We clink glasses and I scull a glass of champagne, the little bubbles of CO_2 fizzing, and almost catching, as they run down my throat.

ALASTAIR CLARKE

chill

took the jerky hours of night
placed on morning's tray

unpositioning this
of unwanted things.

watched birds skittering
while mist shifted over Tararua's

toothed peaks as if unmoving
as if moveless in afternoon's

pale light. words fallen.
this hurt. apples wind-tossed

rotting now on lawn.
now abatement, this unforgetting,

these glottal movements,
tongue searching behind teeth

in breath's familiar rhythm.
to howl? a kind of love?

to remember beneath wind's
whispering the scents in fresh-cut

grass. listening, listening
to the dense rattling of rain

HELENA DE BRES

Sea-dreaming

A dream I have all the time now, the only one I remember on waking up, is about not visiting the sea. In it, I'm on a summer vacation in New Zealand, where I lived till the age of twenty-two. I know the trip is almost over, but whenever I try to check my flight, my mind mists up, my limbs go limp and I can't unlock my phone. I'm half hoping my plane has already left so I can stay longer; I'm also panicking about how expensive that would be, and what I would do about my job back in Boston. All of that is stressful, but it's not what's really working me up. My dream-self has just realised that, though I've been in New Zealand for nearly a month, incredibly I haven't been to the sea.

Though in square footage New Zealand is only slightly bigger than Oregon, it has 15,000 kilometres of coastline, compared with the United States' 20,000. It's basically one very long beach with some cities, towns, mountains and paddocks laid out alongside it. To *not* get to the sea on a summer vacation in New Zealand you have to be creative, wilful and perverse. You have to avoid walking in a straight line, you have to say *no no no* to everyone you love, and each morning after breakfast you have to turn back to your bedroom, enter it, tighten the blinds and slam the door.

In this dream I'm incredulous and outraged, but no longer fully surprised. When you have a recurring dream for long enough, the dream starts to recognise itself mid-course. Your dream-self says both 'I'm doing this *again?*' and 'How *can* I be doing this again, when I even have a regular dream about doing it: a dream in which I remember a dream in which I remember a dream in which ...' I'm so good at berating myself while asleep that, after semi-waking up, I can keep foggily apologising to myself for not visiting the sea for a full ten minutes. I'm contrite, but distraught too, often on the verge of tears. *I can't leave. I won't leave. I need to get to the sea.*

No one wants to hear people talking about their dreams, especially dreams in which the symbolism is this full frontal. Oceans represent everything large and significant and are as subtle as a tsunami. The sea is the subconscious, the sea is the transcendent, the sea is instinct, God, truth, beauty, death—yeah. The sea is whence you came, the sea is whither you'll return. The sea goes in and out: it's your breath, your heartbeat, sex, time's tick and tock. The sea will draw you in (it will kill you), it will spit you back on the beach (it will save you). The sea is the Other, the sea is the Lover, the sea is the real-yet-hidden-you. The sea is everything you're not attending to while you're attending to everything else.

Or maybe the sea is just, well, the sea? A friend of mine has a recurring dream about her teeth falling out. It's a textbook anxiety dream, and my friend is anxious. Thing is, she's anxious in part because her teeth *are* threatening to fall out, according to her periodontist.

I really miss the sea.

*

Boston is officially right by the sea. When you circle over Logan International Airport, what you get from the window is allegedly a harbour view. When you deplane, you can order clam chowder and lobster rolls from what's billed as a 'local seafood' restaurant. If you walk to the eastern edge of Massachusetts, your feet will eventually touch rocks, then sand, then what people like to call 'the Atlantic Ocean'. I've been to the 'port' of Boston, to its northern and southern 'coastline' suburbs, to Cape Cod, which is known as the National 'Seashore'. I've lived in Boston for twenty years now, I've seen all of this many times with my own two eyes, and I still don't believe a word of it.

Some of us suffer from the affliction that the first person we fall in love with comes to define *love object* for us forever, so that later romantic partners don't really count as such, unless they're closely similar to the original type. We universalise too quickly; our love for that first person becomes abstract, and it negates all non-conforming particulars. Who can really love Lou or Alex when Sam = Beloved? Something like this may have happened to me with the New Zealand seashore, starting in 1979.

There are pictures of me and my twin sister sitting upright on an Auckland beach sometime late in that year. We look stupidly happy, the way babies do when they're out in the sun. Our legs are jutting out of our diapers, each chubby section cradled in its own warm trough of sand. We've grasped some of that sand in our pudgy hands and are stuffing it gleefully into our mouths. Floppy hats shade our faces but we're squinting anyway, because we're looking at something that's shifting, smashing and sparkling brighter than anything we've seen before. We throw shells and twigs at each other, pull off our hats in triumph, let ice-cream stream down our chins. 'WHAT'S THAT OUT THERE?' shout our four startled eyes. We can't get over it and we don't want to: we're at the seaside, and in love.

*

My parents both come from major seafaring nations but have radically different attitudes toward the sea. Dad arrived in New Zealand in 1954, on an ocean liner that took five weeks to sail from the Netherlands to Wellington. The front page of the *Dominion* newspaper the next morning featured a photo of him, his parents and his six brothers and sisters, lined up in order of height on the ship's sunny deck. Dad, seven years old, is two-thirds of the way down the line, at some distance from his own father, whose professional summons from God via the Dutch Reform Church had set this grand voyage in motion.

My father, unlike my grandfather, is not what you would ordinarily consider a spiritual man. I've seen him inside a church maybe five times in my life and each time he was clearly dying to get out. But Dad's fervour for the sea is unmistakably religious; it comes with all the core trappings. First: the observance of ritual. From late November to the final stretches of February, on any day the weather is passably fine, Dad can be found taking his swimming togs and towel off the frayed washing line in the laundry and making the five-minute trip to the beach.

Next, shortly afterward: the mortification of the flesh. Wellington's beaches are fed by currents that come directly from Antarctica. Their waters are populated by giant fur seals, well-insulated penguins and the cold-blooded bodies of ancient, alien fish. Even on the sunniest of days, entering the waves on the south coast instantly sends a jolt of paralysing pain from your feet to your skull. You have to steel yourself for a couple of minutes, until your entire body is numb, at which point you can kick back and enjoy it.

Then, most obviously: the devotion. On a warm summer day Dad will take a dip in the morning, sneak in another on the way back from the supermarket, and possibly return for a third in the evening. If you're talking to him at the precise moment that the clouds part a little or a stray sunbeam hits the kitchen counter, a note of distraction will cross his face. You turn your back for a second and he disappears, the gate by the letterbox rattling shut. It's passion, of course, but also, as in any great religion, guilt. 'Why do you do this to yourself?' I asked over the phone one February, after a tale of a particularly energising swim at Lyall Bay. Dad laughed nervously. 'I guess I kind of feel bad if I don't.'

My mother's relationship to the sea is more complicated. She grew up in a suburb of Birmingham, England, in the 1950s. If there was water, it came in teacups or, later, in the river that wound through Oxford, where she trained to be a nurse. That's where Dad met her, as a foreign student in the 1960s. Mum agreed to move to New Zealand with him nine months later; they took a layover in Mauritius on the way. 'The sea was like a bath,' my mother says wistfully of that legendary week.

You might infer that her failure to enter the New Zealand ocean for almost my entire life reduces to an aversion to being cold. But the real problem is that Mum is terrified of swimming: the only way they got her into the water in Mauritius was by getting her drunk and high first. In her early days in New Zealand, Dad managed, somehow, to coax her into the ocean. She was knee deep when a wave descended and knocked her flat. As she tells this story, she lay on the sand under fifteen inches of calm water and told herself: 'Well, I guess this is it. I've had a good life and now I'm going to die.' After a perplexed pause, Dad tapped her on the shoulder, pulled her up with one arm and led her back into the light.

In the yin-yang of my parents' forty-year marriage, Mum is the yin—the mystic, the plumber of the shadows—to Dad's sun-kissed, terrestrial yang. There's always, of course, a little yin in the yang, and Dad's attachment to ocean swimming, as noted, has its otherworldly qualities. But for Mum the sea is almost *all* otherworldly, drenched in its own symbols. She doesn't need to go into the sea physically because she's already in it metaphysically, ninety-nine percent of the time.

That said, Mum is also an artist; she loves beautiful things—and what's more beautiful than the sea? So she likes to sit and look at it, when she can work up the energy to apply the various moisturisers, sunscreens and clothing items needed to shield her British skin from the sun. *The sea is dangerous*, this elaborate prep announces, *but we're going there anyway*! It's part of what I love about my mother, and the sea.

*

'But what kind of sea is it?' my Boston friends ask when I try to explain my problem. 'What's different about it?'

'Well, it's very cold,' I say. 'And it has coves. And rocks.'

'Like Maine, you mean?'

'*Kiiiind* of,' I say, meaning absolutely not.

'Like Northern California? Or the Oregon coast?'

'*More* like that, but ...'

They slam a hand upon the table. 'You should try this place I found on the North Shore last summer. You're going to love it!'

I wince. They always get to this move—*don't give up, you just haven't found the right beach yet*—and they're always wrong. I feel more alienated from them at this point than I do at any other time. They seem impregnable suddenly, self-sufficient, forbiddingly sea-satisfied. I begin to wonder whether they have hearts at all, or if there's a great cavity inside them where the sea should be.

But I admit I'm not articulating myself very well. I incline urgently toward them in a final desperate attempt.

'It's like that thing Montaigne said when his best friend died,' I say. 'You know? If you press me to say why I loved him, I can only say: because it was him, because it was me?'

'Hmm, okay,' they blink distantly, like a lighthouse on the Eastern 'seaboard'.

I can see they're done with the subject. I'm not.

*

One of the great memories of my childhood—one of those iconic, composite ones that no longer attaches to any particular moment but has come to sum up a whole period of life—is of our family at the beach. Mum, complexion fortified and elegantly hatted, is sitting on the picnic blanket up on the dunes at Princess Bay. It's unclear how long she'll stay there before retreating to the car because the wind is vicious. But for the moment there she is, shading her eyes and looking out toward the South Island, thinking about who knows what.

My sister and I have followed Dad down the dunes, his worn jandals flapping in front of us, our heels sinking into the cooler layers of sand under the hot surface, sending out fountains and avalanches on both sides. When we get to the water's edge Dad plunges straight in, while Julia and I take the sectional approach, screaming at each successive partial submersion.

We've brought our junior diving gear, so at the penultimate stage we suction our masks to our faces and bite down resolutely on our snorkels. Then, in a flurry of panic, we launch ourselves off the sandy surface into the green and purple forest a few metres in. We kick furiously over to the rocks to warm up, and to fight the waves threatening to sweep us back to shore. We can see Dad's pale body hovering over an underwater valley, his hand pointing to a school of silver spotties threading through the seaweed. We three swim like a school of fish ourselves, heading off together in one direction, adjusting as a wave slams in, taking individual adventures, then returning to report on our treasures. We surface, adjust the masks, Mum waves from high up on the beach. Everyone is in their proper place, no one is missing, no one wants to be anywhere else.

While the period attached to that memory feels endless to me, in reality it only lasted about five years, from 1986 to around 1991. When Julia and I became teenagers, various forces seemed to stand in the way of our easy access to the ocean. We became self-conscious about our bodies, worried about being seen with wet hair, or sandy faces, or in our togs. We cared, suddenly, about what people other than Dad might think. We became more physically sensitive, squeamish about being painfully cold. We had other things to do—homework to complete, plans to make, friends to meet in town. We still swam sometimes, but just as often we sat beside the sea, like Mum, often alone, pining over some boy.

One might have hoped this finicky stage would end, and maybe it would have, if other factors hadn't intervened. In our twenties, Julia moved to landlocked Luxembourg and I moved to a city next to a sea I don't believe in. I refuse to swim in the ocean near Boston; I stick to ponds and pools, which are humble enough to not try to be something they're not. When I go back to New Zealand on vacation, every couple of years, I usually do swim in the sea but find myself overthinking it. 'Is it worth it?' I ask myself beforehand, the teenage self resurfacing. Then, once I'm in: 'Why can't I have this all the time?'

Thirty years ago, neither question would have made sense.

*

Recently I told Julia about my dream about not visiting the sea. She said she had exactly the same dream, over in Luxembourg, regularly.

'Do you ever actually get there in the dream?' I asked.

'No,' she said.

'Is it one of those things where, if we did get there, we'd die in our sleep?'

'Probably,' she said. 'It's like dreams about dying. You definitely don't want to die in a dream.'

I went online immediately after this call to check how widespread our dream is. The first Google link for 'common recurring dreams' reports the results of a survey recently conducted by a bed manufacturer. Falling is number one on the list (53.5 percent), having your teeth fall out number nine (27.3 percent). The sea doesn't make an appearance at all in the Top 35, though drowning appears at number 29.

I called Julia back to report that people in general are not dreaming about not visiting the sea.

'It's weird,' I said. 'Like, isn't it obvious? The sea is so figuratively loaded. Every human desire is attached to it somehow. Shouldn't every dream basically be about the sea?'

Julia claimed that you only thought the sea was metaphorically everything if you had grown up by the sea. For other people, something else played the role of everything. 'What do they dream about, those people?' Julia asked.

Edna St Vincent Millay, an exile from the coast of Maine, asked the same question in her 1921 poem 'Inland'. Of people who build their houses inland, she writes, with pity, 'What do they long for, as I long for/ One salt smell of the sea once more?' I'd forgotten till I went back to it that this poem is about a recurring dream. Millay is 'starting up in [her] inland bed':

> Beating the narrow walls, and finding
> Neither a window nor a door,
> Screaming to God for death by drowning—
> One salt taste of the sea once more?

I want to believe that wanting so badly to get to the sea, even if you never get there, means you never really left it. But when you're not physically near the sea, your presence at its side is a tough case to make. Maybe this is what our having this dream is about. The sea doesn't register minor gestures; with the ocean, you have to go big. You need to want over and over, you need to want till you're gasping, or the intensity of your devotion will remain in doubt.

There's only so much wanting you can decently do in daylight, but at nighttime you can want all you like. So that's when we sea-dreamers must do the bulk of the labour necessary to make the sea take us seriously. We're working, every night, in the drama of sleep, to recoup our losses, to say we didn't mean it, to say we're back now. What a great kindness, what a merciful benediction it would be, if, by that sheer excess of wanting, we could somehow make it so.

DAVID EGGLETON

Ghost Town

You look a million dollars, old house;
and they say you're worth it,
flossied up with the spit and shine
of brochure talk; you've got it licked,
summery in a dun climate.
The finest music in the world is
korimako calling from a kōwhai tree,
jingle of harness descending the coast road,
belling of a stag like a hunting horn,
the pleasant din of dinner knives,
scrape of lightning-quick forks,
rattle of a hob kettle on the coal range,
church bells, chimes of clocks, horse hooves,
the rolling of iron-clad carriage wheels,
the shriek of a train whistle.
Moonlight's a ghost town—
silent the grass, silent the sky,
silent the alley, silent the house.

GRACE YEE

What Remains

The new normal is off-leash. It barrelled across the ocean at the speed of two white-settler nations on uncharted territory.

⋆

Her entire life she's been off the boat at the vanity in the corner twisting taps: eyes shining, straightening the circular mirror, reaching for glasses not there on the bedside.

It's winter now and she speaks hourly of the revolution seventy years past: the water table shifting, her ankles chalk, her memories an ungainly rack of antlers cracking the parietal bones in her skull.

⋆

Despite serious seismological questions, the sea wall gives them a false sense of security. Their demise is a fault buried deep beneath the salt. There are no precise forecasts.

Every morning he walks a warm apple pie and a loaf of fresh bread in a brown paper bag damp with steam, newspaper tucked under his arm. The kettle boils and the windows fog white. She plays *Für Elise* on the Yamaha upstairs. He salutes the lions, falls asleep, World News on his belly.

When the plates shudder, they stand together in the middle of the room, her eyes fixed on a peeling hibiscus, his on the ceiling beams. Afterwards they still the swinging lamps together, respirations calm despite cardiovascular complications (her arrhythmia, his congested ventricles), blood on the walls stung violet.

⋆

At 4am I recognise his wide-legged gait near the red brick chapel and I say, *No Dad. Go back.* The windows may look pretty but your lenses are opaque and your maculae degenerate. You know she is unfit for climbing on roofs, that while she may be harmless, she is not unharmed. You know how the cages are stacked and that domesticated is not the same as docile, that sooner or later the ground will stop sliding, silence will gong, and out on the street there'll be nothing to see but grey sky between the houses and the trees and the lampposts, what remains when the ocean is sucked out to sea.

BRENT KININMONT

Hong Kong 1997

1. Swim!

The bouncy castle has taken off
with the child inside. The long-haired mother

cannot throw a line of herself
across that ever-widening moat of clouds.

Apart from the grinning creatures (pigs,
a wolf) inflated on the walls

the stronghold had been empty of others
to bump against. From this far now

it could be a birthday cake;
for burning candles, the orange turrets.

And that gust still trying to blow out
a child's diminishing reward

for not fussing in the mall, not touching
anything that might have punctured her.

2. The Saved

He was made to go to Sunday school.
But across her primary years he makes

the child swim. She might one day
travel widely, and Bible lessons

won't save her from the sinking
ferries in his head. In that crowded

public pool she gets faster at the crawl,
practices breaststroke when

kicking feet get in the way.
He won't let her quit until she's swum

a hundred lengths without pausing,
while cleanly palming at the end of lanes

that vivid cross of blue tiles
just below the waterline.

3. Father Tongue
A firm grasp had taken her far.
From across the ocean she admitted

she was staying put. *So be it!*—
the feeble words he huffed

before hanging up.
They sounded like *Soviet*:

someone from a bygone union.
He wonders now, had she noticed the echo?

Her mother somehow held her tongue
when he spilled the bottle

he'd been wading through,
then wiped the table with the dinner mats.

The daughter had embroidered them
with all the letters of his alphabet.

4. One-child Policy
Across the pond the wind has swept
the swan boats into a jam.

Those stuck in the middle
are sheltered from the spray.

They'll gain traction when the fringe
scatters. But people on the edge

are still pedalling in place!
Neck and neck, couples

and small families going nowhere.
Swimming out is not an option—

the signs are clear on this.
One soaked woman cradling a child

has reached her limit. *See!*
It's only up to her knees.

BILL DIREEN

Willi Fels*

Who are you, Willi Fels
with your name of rock?

In so many museums
I have recurred,
as if born anew,

and often in small letters
a name recurs, a benefactor.
Here it is yours,

Willi Fels,
I learn it as I pass
vestiges of determinant periods,

black images on clay
light lines on fired black backgrounds,
marble scraps,

vases reassembled,
as if history has apologetically
and over a new century

glued together the casualties
of its stupidity and terror.
You gave these things

you touched and read,
to us who live so much
in the virtual.

I grew in the virtual of radio,
of slides and other copies,
and from the 21st century of the console,

of the cluster, of the bubble
I think of you in your 19th century
of plaster moulds, mezzotints and pianoforte.

You rescued originals
intended for son Harold,
blown apart fighting your ancestors,

and remitted to us purchases
or finds of provident fortune,
so that some pandemic Sunday

a casual visitor may leave a wintrous Dunedin
and sense
what we can never know.

* Willi Fels (1858–1946) was a prominent German merchant, philanthropist and collector who settled in Dunedin and became managing director of Hallenstein Brothers, established by his father-in-law, Bendix Hallenstein. When Fels' only son, Harold, was killed in action in October 1917 he decided to leave his extensive collection of 80,000 pieces to the Otago Museum. Fels inspired a love of artistic and intellectual interests in others, including his grandson, poet and editor Charles Brasch.

PETRA NYMAN

Superheroes

The trees rush past us, casting shadows over the road. We're excited cos Dad has come with us today. He's driving faster than Mum would, and it makes the game harder. Dad is a rally driver and we are superheroes. We're not scared of anything. He smiles at us in the rear-view mirror and turns the radio up. We giggle and shake our dangling legs to the rhythm of the music.

Mum sits quietly in the passenger seat. She reaches to the cigarette lighter in the centre of the car and pushes it in. Then her hands dive inside her bag and fish out a packet of smokes. She's wearing a white blouse and reminds me of Popeye with a cigarette hanging from the corner of her mouth. The lighter pops out; Mum touches it carefully to the tip of the cigarette. A red glow crawls from the metal to the white paper and begins to eat through it. The car fills with smoke before she inches her window down a crack, just enough for it wriggle out, like a genie escaping out of a bottle. I turn my head to look out the window and see a hawk gliding over an oat field that glows golden in the late summer sun.

'Something beginning with H,' I call out.

My sister searches for an answer out her window.

'Horse?'

'N-ahh.'

'Hare?'

'Nope.'

'Hungry cow?'

We all laugh. Except for Mum. I see Dad glance at her, but she turns her head away. My sister missed the bird.

Dad takes a ramp off the highway and Mum flicks the end of her cigarette out of the window before we pull up outside a petrol station. I love the sweet smell of petrol and open my door to let it creep in. My sister makes gagging noises and holds her nose. Mum tells me to close the door. Dad walks back towards the car and sees me watching him. He slips between the pumps and pretends to get stuck to make me laugh. When he gets back in the car he passes a bag of sweets to me and my sister over the seat without turning.

'Travel candy,' he says and smiles in the mirror.

Mum gives him a look, but says nothing. He laughs and she shakes her head.

'What?' he says with a changed tone. 'Can't a father treat his kids once in a while?'

'Sure he can,' Mum answers and turns to look at us with a vacant smile. She tucks her hair behind her ear, exposing the corner of her eye. It's turned purple now. Then she turns to look out her window again.

Us kids, we sit in silence, mouths full of sweetness, as the car merges back into traffic. Suddenly, Dad begins to laugh and we ask him what's funny. He says it's his lucky day. We say how come. He pulls a scratch-card out of his shirt pocket and waves it in the air between the two front seats for us to see, like he did with the sweets before.

'What is it, Dad?' my sister asks.

'I turned a mark into twenty just like that!'

He snaps his fingers and the card floats in the air for a moment before settling on the floor underneath our feet. He laughs some more, then steps on the gas and the car flies forward. Me and my sister cheer from the back seat. We think we'll be rich. We think everything is going to be okay. Our bodies sway together when we go around corners, the seatbelts digging into our stomachs like we are being cut in half, but we giggle, hold our hands up in the air and pretend we are in a rollercoaster.

'Slow down,' Mum says quietly.

Dad ignores her and she goes back to being silent. We zoom ahead and pass every car going our way. We are the fastest.

'Are we the leaders?' I ask Dad every time the road is clear ahead of us.

'We are the leaders!' he hollers.

Our car has wings and can fly. Our car is magic. Our car takes us over the treetops and across the fields. Our car is the best car in the world. Our car is the fastest of all. Until the silver car comes along.

We glide past it at first, cheering over our victory, but then it catches us up and takes the lead again. Dad taps the steering wheel and lets out a roar like he's a wild animal.

'Don't,' Mum says.

'Hold on,' Dad says, glancing at us in the mirror.

We pass the silver car and again take the lead. The road is ours once more. Dad winds down his window all the way and the breeze blows hair into our eyes.

'We can't see!' we call out. He pokes his head out the window and howls like a wolf. Then winds it back up. We clap, and make up a song about being the fastest car on the road. But Mum turns and gives us the eye so we go silent. Then a flash of silver flies past us again.

Mum looks at Dad and says, 'Please don't, the girls are in the back.'

Her voice trembles and it scares us, but Dad drives even faster. We are in the lead again and he is a howling wolf. We wait for his laughter, but it doesn't come any more. We stop cheering. We stop playing our game. We know he's in a mood now, so we don't make a peep.

The silver car tries to pass us again, but this time it only makes it beside us. I look over and see young men spilling out of its windows, arms waving in the wind like streamers. Their mouths are moving fast, they are yelling something, but I can't make out the words. Dad keeps his eyes on the road like they are not there at all.

'Slow down,' Mum says again. 'Let them pass!'

But he doesn't. The silver car hovers beside us for what feels like forever until it finally drops back behind us.

None of us says a word. I concentrate on the sunlight flickering through the tree trunks as we race past a forest and I feel dizzy. Then I recognise the smell of the paper mill. I look at my sister and take her hand. I squeeze it and whisper *nearly there*. Grandma will have lunch ready. She'll be in the kitchen fussing about, setting the table for all of us. Thinking of her makes me feel safe.

*

The sky is clear blue when we pull up outside Grandma's apartment building. I see her through the car window. She is standing on her balcony on the third floor and waving at us with a smile. The building is white and the way the sun gleams off its shell hurts my eyes, but I keep looking up towards her anyway. Dad winds his window down and I lean forward, calling out to her. We made it. As soon as the car stops, I jump out and wave to Grandma with both hands. I forget all about being scared.

Mum is getting our backpacks from the boot when I see a flash of silver. The car glides past us and stops a little way away. Dad is still in the driver's seat. He's rolling a cigarette. He doesn't smoke ready-mades; he says they are for women and lazy bastards. I see the men get out of their car and I pull on Mum's top.

'I'm getting them,' she says.

But I say: 'Mum!'

She turns and sees the men; they are striding towards our car. One of them is holding a bat in his hand.

'Inside!' Mum screams.

She grabs my sister, who is crouching by a drain dropping pebbles in it, and starts running towards the building with my sister under her arm like a bag of potatoes, and I run too. I want to scream and call for Dad to run as well, but no sound comes out of my mouth. I hear a thud, before the hallway door clicks shut behind us.

Mum drags me behind her but I look back through the glass doors and see Dad scamper out of the car and the men's mouths moving wide open and shut again, their bodies leaning towards Dad. Mum pulls me deeper into the hallway and I can't see out any more.

Usually, me and my sister fight over who gets to press the button for the elevator but we are not fighting now, or taking the elevator. My sister is swallowing sobs in Mum's arms. I climb up the twirly stairs behind her. Then Grandma appears above us. She's rushing down the stairs to meet us and reaches out to my hand, pulling me up even faster.

When we're inside her apartment Grandma slams the door shut and fastens the safety chain. Mum collapses behind the door with my sister in her arms. I'm sobbing now too, but Mum just shakes her head. She hugs my sister tight. I want her to hug me too, but Grandma pulls me in and squashes me against her apron. She smells like meatballs.

The clock ticks on the wall and Grandma hums a song, holding me tight towards her. In the painting on the wall a guardian angel watches over two children on a bridge. Finally we hear sirens. I try to move towards the balcony but Grandma won't let me go. Mum puts my sister down, tells us to stay with

Grandma, and gets to her feet. We follow her with our eyes as she disappears into the living room. We know she's going out to the balcony.

Grandma takes me and my sister to the kitchen. She sits us at the table and pours both of us a glass of milk. Then she takes out two bowls from the cupboard and opens the freezer. She pulls out an ice-cream carton and slices it with a knife like it's a loaf of bread. She places a bowl of ice-cream and a spoon each in front of us. My sister's eyes light up; she doesn't think about what's going on outside any more and digs in. I watch the steam rising from the potatoes in the middle of the table.

Mum will walk in any minute to tell us everything is all right. I know she will. Grandma sits down between us. I hear the clock tick on the wall again, otherwise only silence. The ice-cream begins to melt in my bowl. I lift the spoon and scoop some into my mouth even though I don't really want to. I can't taste anything, but I like how the cold begins to numb my tongue. My sister is sitting across the table from me. When I look up, I see that she's smiling.

BARBARA ELSE

Three Ways to Go

Bury me with a piece of cheese
    in case I need protein in the afterlife
    find me a possum fur hat
    don't forget beads
    nor an oar
    in case there's a river

~

Wrap me with scarves of many colours
    dig a hole in a stretch of green land
    plant over me a maple
    with a trunk like a wand carried
    by one of those elves of Tolkien's
    who sift around
    between his long paragraphs

~

Tip my ashes in a tidy pile
    on the brink of a cliff
    stand back with an excellent wine
    till the wind hurtles up
    invisible fingers flicking spirals
    everywhere
    singing   *now*
                gone

~~~
~~~

JILLY O'BRIEN

Kōtare

You can get to the Portobello dairy the Hoopers Inlet way hugging the gravel but I wouldn't say it's *the* way because the only reason to go is to check firstly that he is waiting and secondly to see him timing his crossing for maximum effect like beautiful things tend to do. When I was sixteen I knew a man called Hugo whose brother Benedict was searching for a forever girl that nobody else would find attractive but whom he adored. She left little glass phials of liquid smells about their flat that were never from rosebuds or lavender or liquorice which seems less romantic now than it was then and I wonder if beautiful things are so because they have impeccable timing.

Downsizing

When my black child-dog died, every morning for some weeks afterwards my mum greeted the imposter bin-bag napping in the dog corner instead, full of something or other, saved Christmas wrapping/ washed cartons honey stacked/ folded crosswords/ phone messages on felt pen run out in lime, dried up in brown on the backs of envelopes from the insurance. Benchtop crockery towers piled crooked piled clean should mean the cupboards are empty unless they hung on to multiple sets from houses that echo and moan which would explain all the chairs waiting downstairs and the loft as a place we never went. Certainly you could sit down after shifting towels and leaflets, always a salt cellar on the piano—intentional and due to overflowing rather than forgetting—this is not a dementia poem. At night you can't see the dog although sniffing will usually pinpoint location, asleep on a life-raft of chairs in heavy seas.

MAITREYABANDHU

Arrival at Pukerua Bay

On this island specialising in ice-cream
and lamb, the green glare and the blue, an island
walkable as Bashō's island strung with shrines
and miracles but upside down—warm north,
a far, snow-muffled south—history
(it seems) is less ambitious, more peaceable:
pocket-sized valleys, pint-sized hills
gem set in a surprisingly moody sea.
The view—a train going one way up
a hill with hot cars, bonnet to bumper, going
the other—seems gathered into the illusion
of being cared for, of being cared about.
So is the astonishment we feel, Gary,
the girls and I, the sea?—its maritime
modalities—or the summery shock of sparrows
after winter's songlessness? And could this be
what rebirth feels like, coming around next to
a bank of nasturtiums, eavesdropping on
the neat crash and folding sound of waves?
I doubt it. I imagine somewhere more apt:
a lime tree high street; a narrow yard with puddles;
an older brother kicking a football, again
and yet again, against a garage wall.

Seahorses and Contrails

The girls are laughing upstairs, being sisters
for a while, while beyond incongruous
Christmas lights the rain dissolves the island
that arrived just yesterday in gull-scurry
and almost flippant cloud. Something is always
being asserted—silver side or shadow,
a cormorant's flight across leviathan waves—
so we can never be here entirely, the eye
taking preference over the ear, taste
for a moment blinding sight, then sound again
asserting ancient rights: the ocean noisy
like the noise of thought, or the bed
thought rises up from hapless to express
that unity beyond this botch of parts.
Ria calls me. As I look up, my mind
suspended between heaven and earth, content
with neither, is like the far horizon's rope.

PHILIP ARMSTRONG

The Advancement of Learning

Day breaks on the internet
with pictures sent back from the New Horizons probe
of Ultima Thule, an icy head and thorax
at the farthest orbit of the sun,

accompanied by a popup of my dream
vacation house, which I've never searched for
and instantly book.

They say Aristotle had a hive made of glass
for studying bees, but the insects
smeared the inner sides with clay.

JANIS FREEGARD

too late for the manatees

the end of days was sometimes delightful:
the sea lapped the shore gentle as a moth sipping sap
otters held paws at night to keep from drifting
we turned to each other, said: *let's fiddle while Rome burns*

everything was on fire, or drowning
it was too late for the manatees
we said: *we saw this coming, we've known for decades,*
we did what we could

the skies were every colour
new landmasses were revealed
we watched evacuations on our devices
saying: *at least we don't have children*

people still wrote songs and planted lettuces
the mountains were overrun with billionaires
we searched clouds for our parents' faces
remembered giraffes

in the evenings we pretended,
saying: *something will take over after us*
maybe the tardigrades—they could hardly do worse
and held on tightly, braced against the drifting

SIONE MONŪ

Joy-Making

1. *Ao' Kakala Mask*, 2022, digital print on smooth cotton rag, 594 x 420mm
2. *Manu Vaea*, 2017, digital print, 841 x 594mm
3. *Rosylyn Monū*, 2017, digital print, 841 x 594mm
4. *Ao' Kakala Mask*, 2022, digital print on smooth cotton rag, 594 x 420mm
5. *Kanokupolu Portrait Two*, 2020, digital print on smooth cotton rag, 420 x 297mm
6. *Kanokupolu Portrait Three*, 2020, digital print on smooth cotton rag, 420 x 297mm
7. *Early Spring*, 2021, digital print on smooth cotton rag, 594 x 420mm
8. *Only Yesterday*, 2020, screenshot from video work commissioned by CIRCUIT AFV for AURA Festival of Artist Moving Images

This suite of photographs explores Sione Monū's work with nimamea'a tui kakala, the traditional Tongan art of flowercraft that is used to produce kahoa, or garlands and cloud forms. Yet, while tradition is central to their practice, Monū's images push for a certain experimentalism, challenging the viewer to think about the convergences between the traditional craft and contemporary settings and materials. Plastic flower and bead kahoa adorn a couch-sitter in a South Auckland upstairs flat, or are worn in combination with Adidas trackies. These images, and Monū's practice in general, reflect the current identity of the Tongan diaspora in Aotearoa with an infectious joy and playfulness. Follow @sione_has_doubts

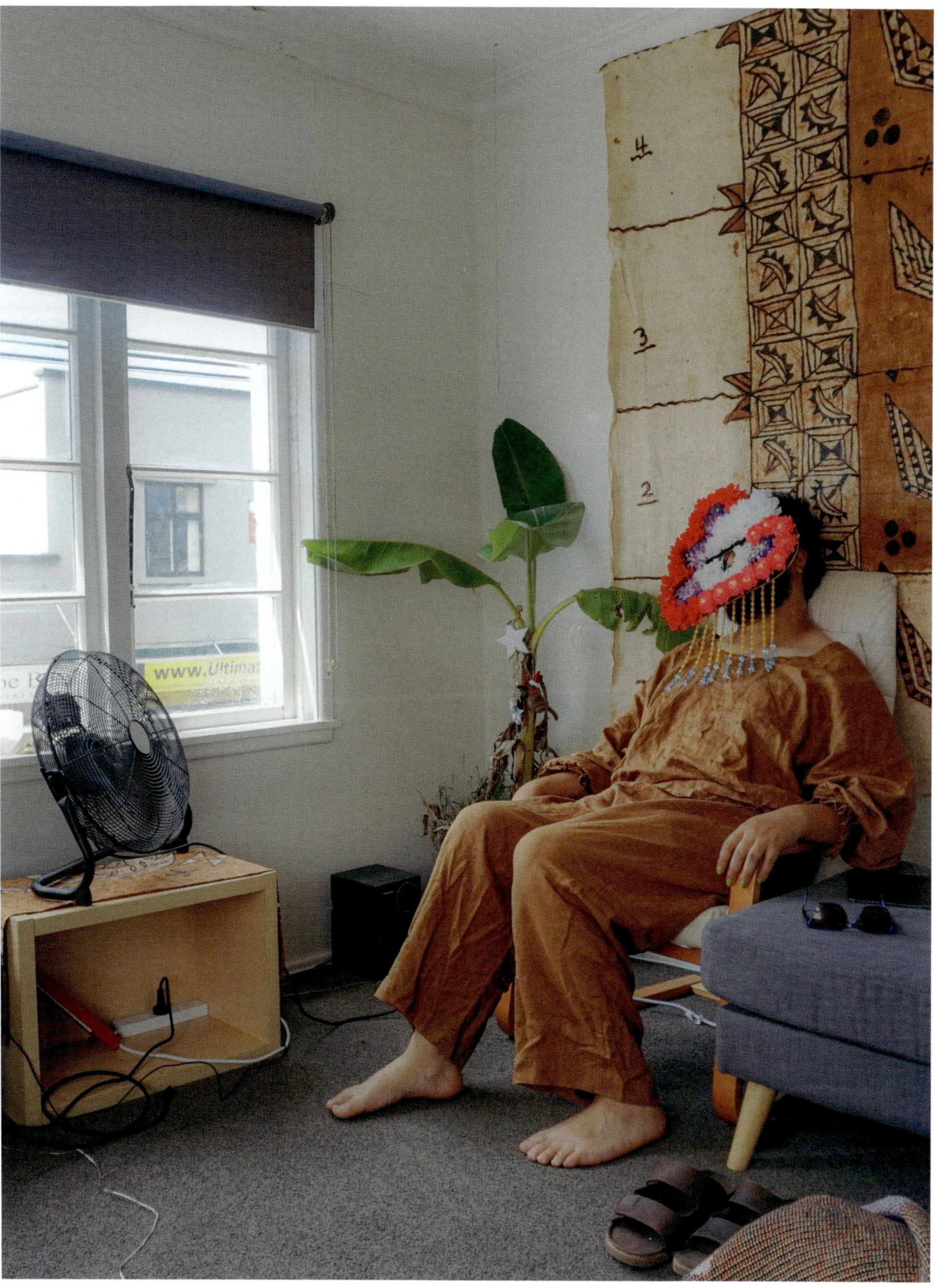

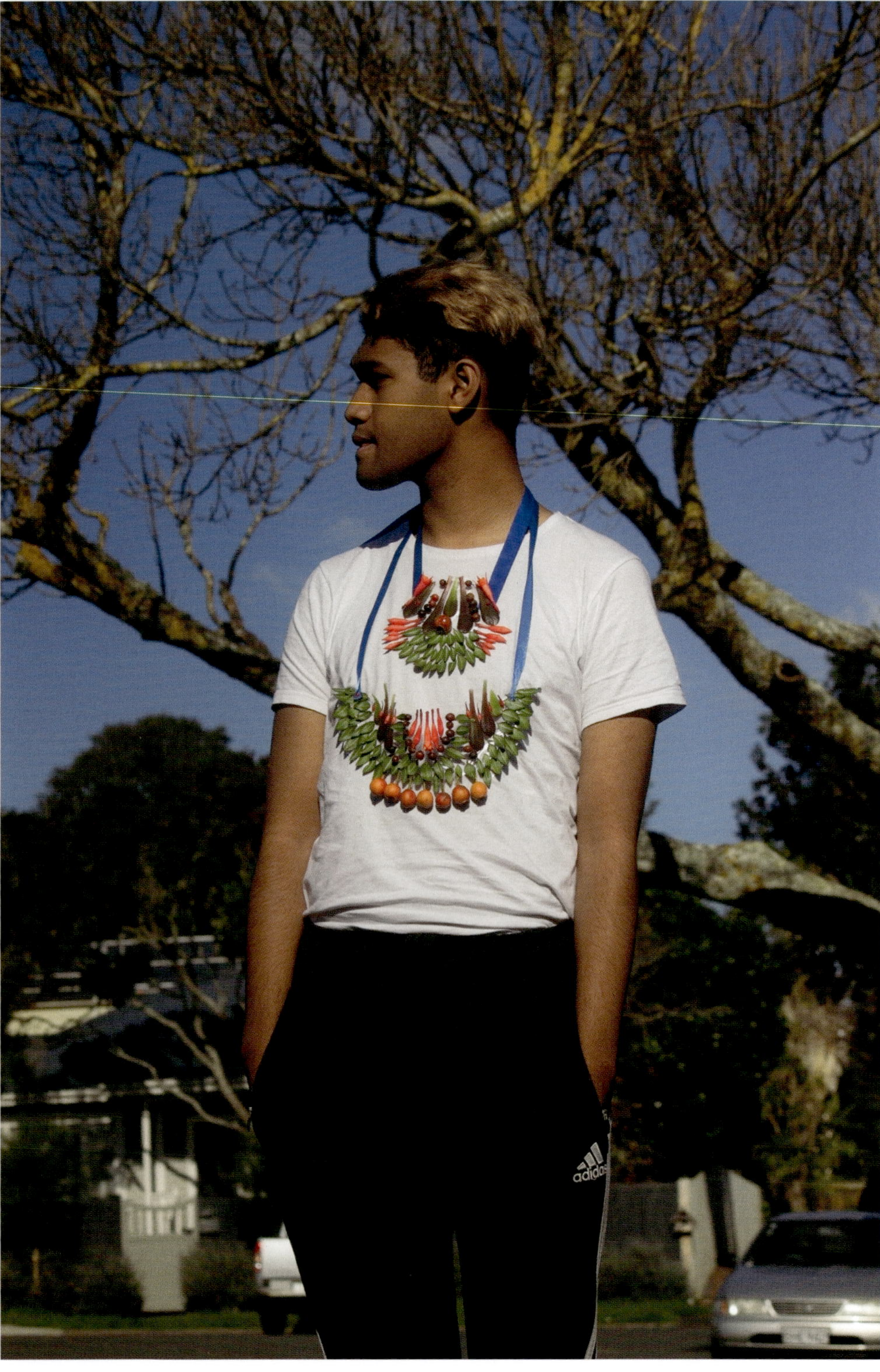
adidas

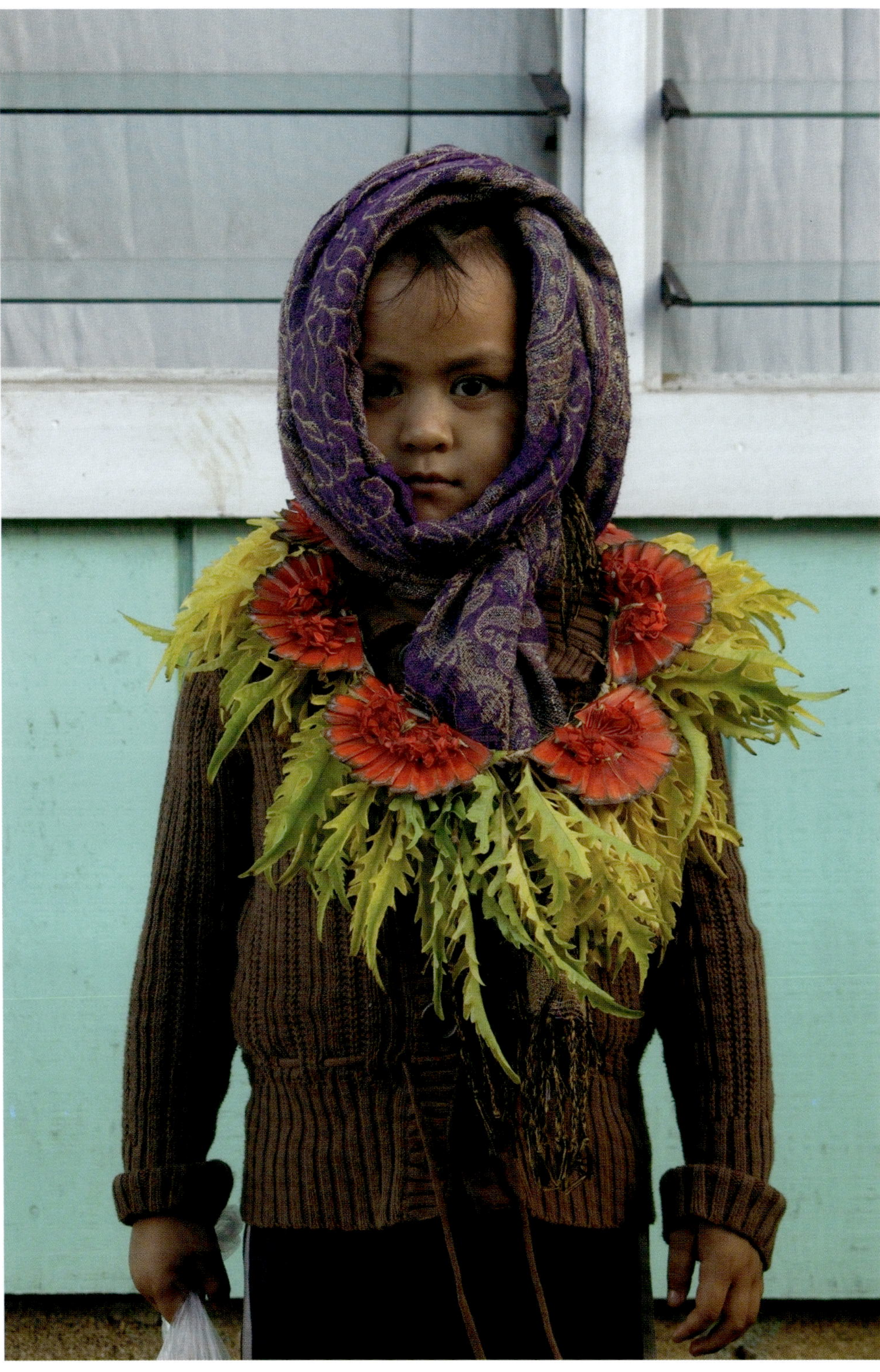

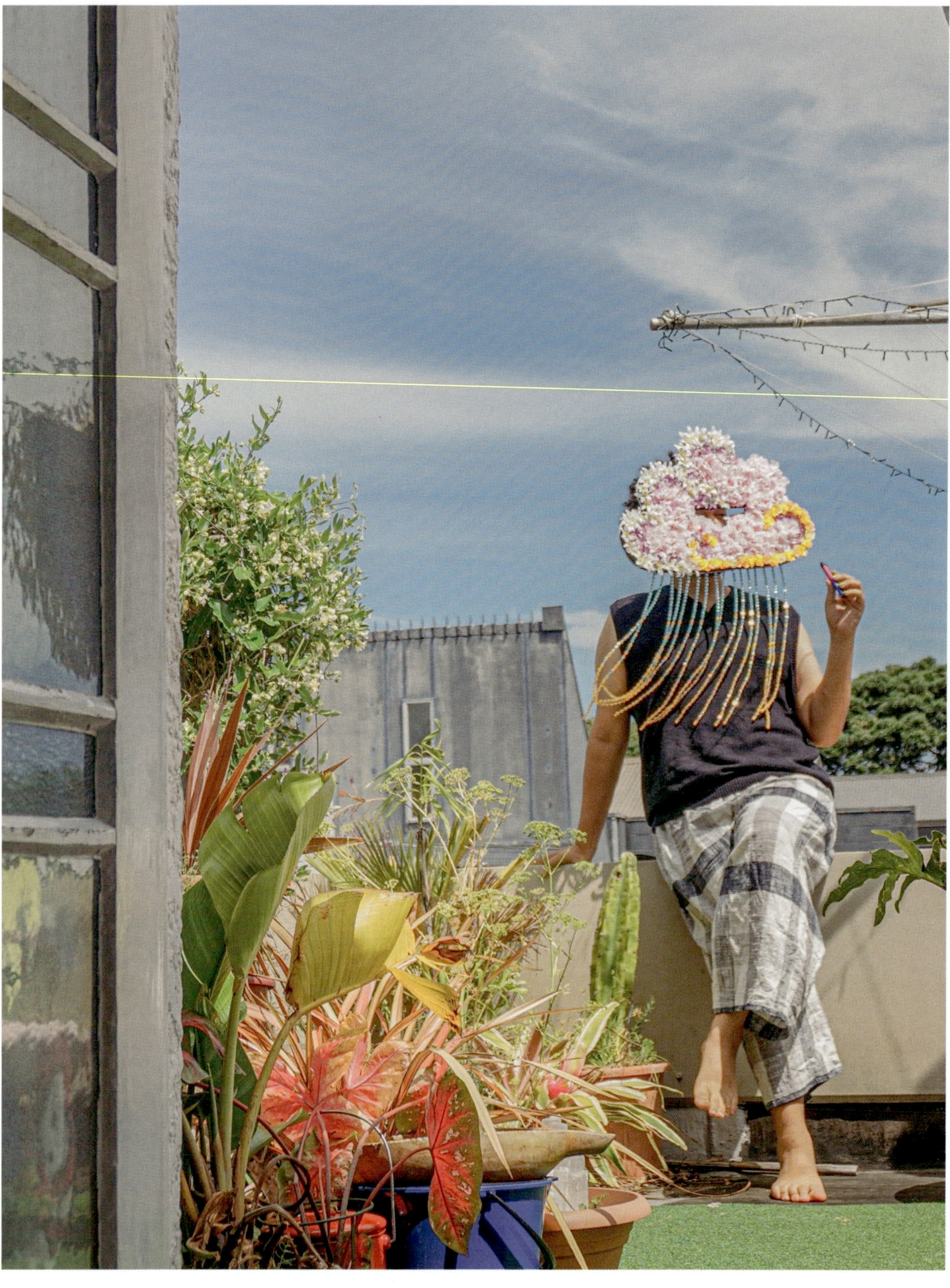

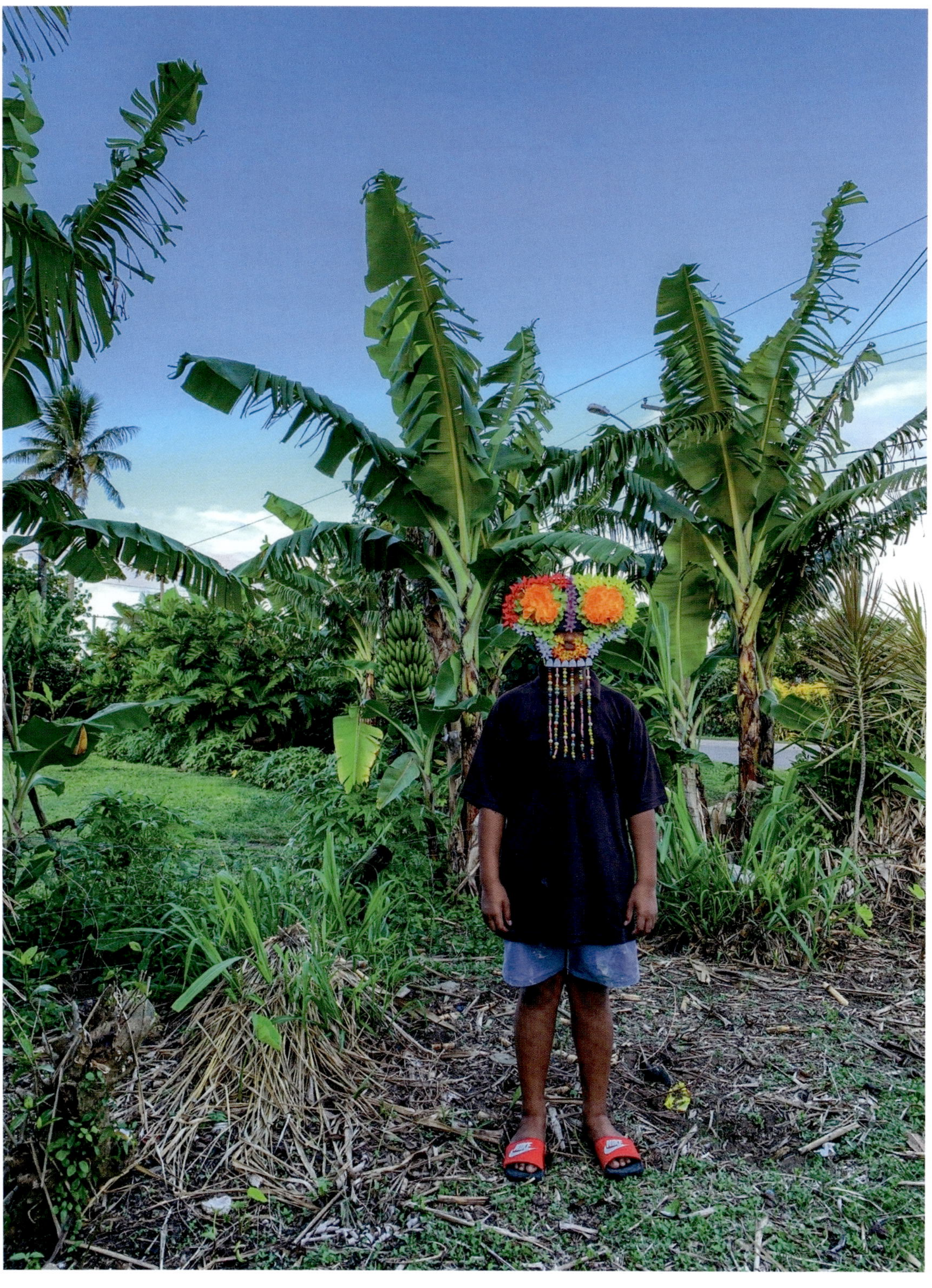

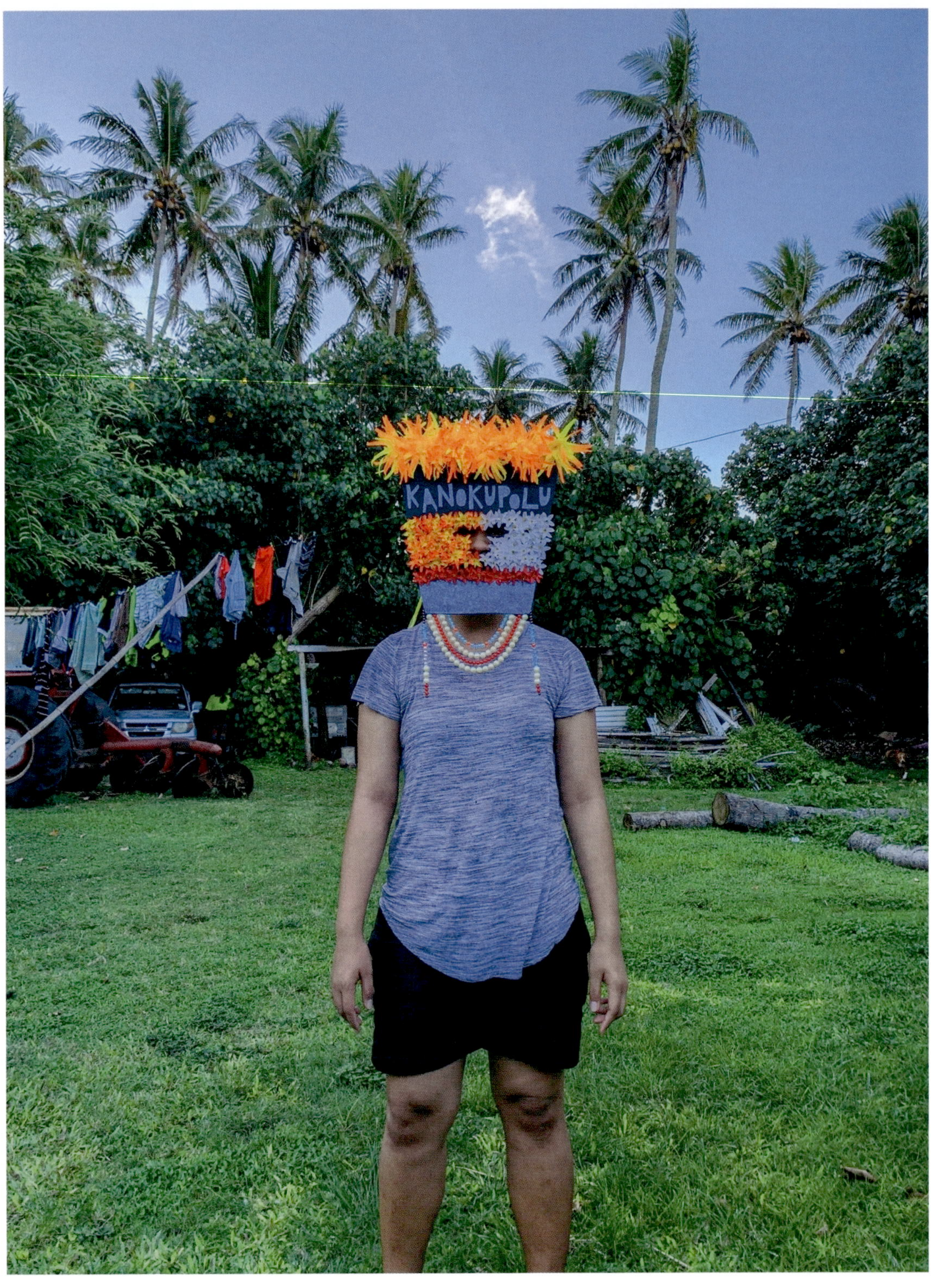
KANOKUPOLU

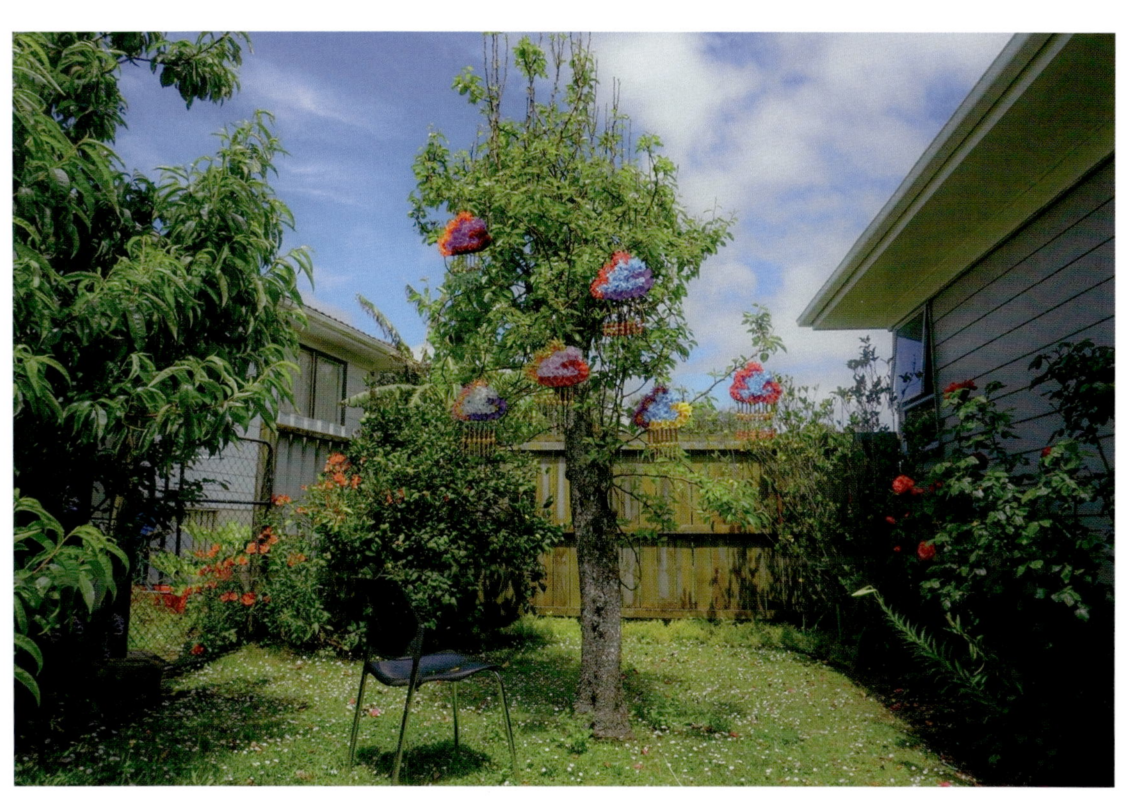

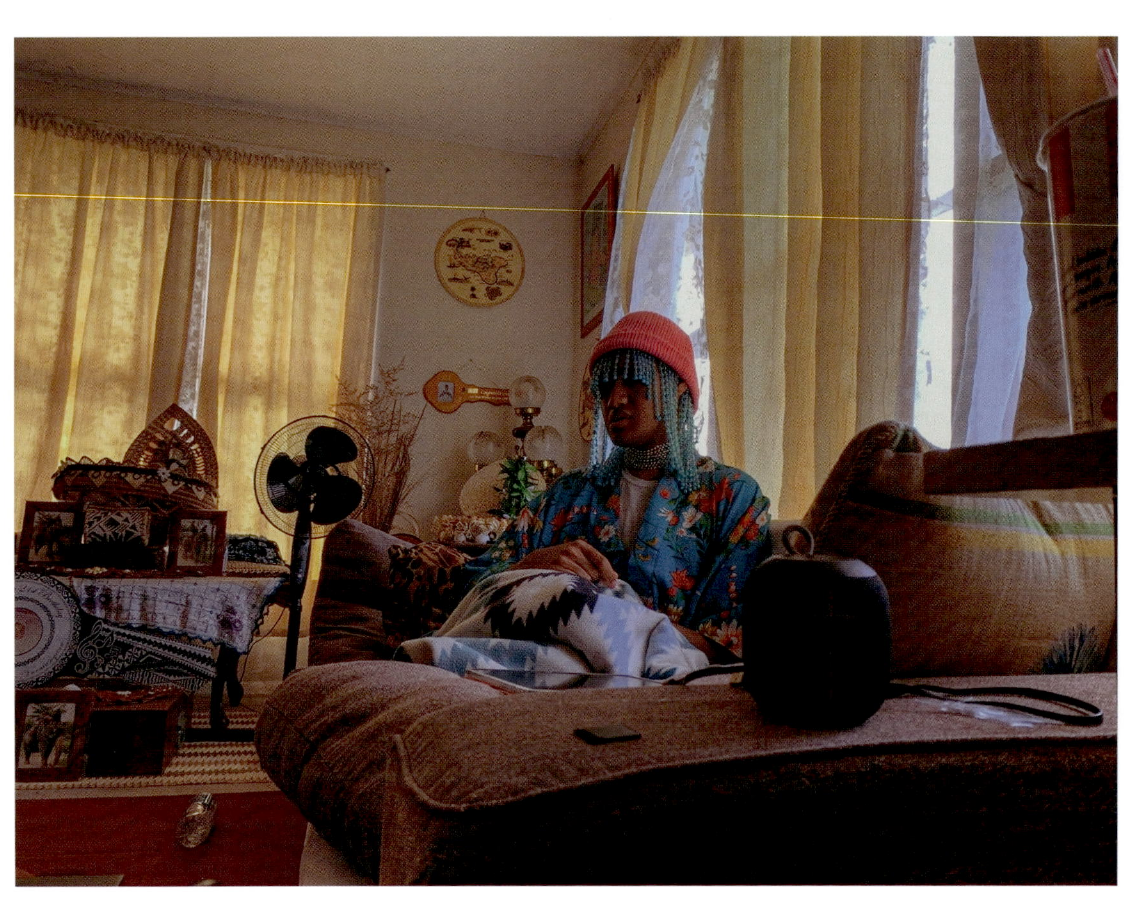

PIP ROBERTSON

Honeymoon in a Town Called Fog

We could have seen the sunset from the house, but it was the first night and Peter insisted we went down the long zigzag path to the beach.

It was spring. Holiday homes were boarded up, restaurants closed. The few people on the beach were outnumbered by the dogs. Three came and sat near us, attentive. I rolled up my jeans and walked down to the water. It was freezing and I only got ankle deep. Glossy kelp shifted with the waves. It could have been a west coast beach at home, and I tried to convince myself we were somewhere it was possible to relax.

When I sat down next to Peter, he passed me a paper bag.

'Empanadas. I bought them from some Argentinians raising cash to get home.' He nodded towards a couple further down the beach.

'That was charitable. Any good?'

Peter tilted his head, non-committal. I bit into gluey dough and raw onion, and spat it out.

'They didn't cost much,' he said, digging his toes into the sand.

'Well, we don't have much.'

I threw the empanadas to the dogs. They gulped them down, tails rotating with gratitude. The sunset, in spite of it all, was spectacular.

'Happy honeymoon,' I said, and neither of us was sure if I was being sarcastic.

We hadn't been paying enough attention to the world. We were busy in churches with gory Jesuses in cities at breath-zapping altitudes. Then we were off grid in the thick heat of the jungle. We woke every day to raucous birds and howler monkeys. We saw wallowing capybaras and the rump of a tapir disappearing through the trees. A sloth blinked down at us in what felt like mutual wonder. Our guide pointed out jaguar prints on the path and said it was a lucky sign.

Then, back in a hotel room with reception, our phones chirped with messages. A world map bloomed with infections. A final flight home was leaving but it was thousands of miles away and there was no way we could make it in time. But, convinced it couldn't really be the last flight, we spent 38 hours on a series of buses, rented a one-room apartment near the airport, and called the airline every day.

The airline couldn't say when the next flight might be. At first we thought they meant which day of the week. We realised they meant which month. Our original departure date came and went. For outings, we put on masks and joined the supermarket queues patrolled by armed police. For time alone, I went into the bathroom. Even sighs were audible through the flimsy door.

Peter found the house online. It was high on a hill overlooking the sea.

'It's above a town called Niebla. That means fog.' He'd been the more diligent attendee at the night classes.

He called the landlord and we caught the bus south the same day. Fog wasn't on our itinerary. It was somewhere cheap and quiet to wait until we could leave and have our lives back.

We returned from the sunset to find ants all over the fruit bowl, the table, the rubbish bin, the dishes by the sink. There was a trail along the windowsill and a scrum by the fridge. They gave off a sharp, raisiny smell as I wiped them off the benchtop.

Peter trekked back down to the store in the town and returned bearing a box with a picture of an ant in a top hat, posing like Fred Astaire.

'Is that to kill them, or make them dance?'

'It says poison. It's all they had.'

The idea was the ants drank it, then carried it back to the nest in their bellies, like unwitting suicide bombers. We filled the plastic dishes that came in the box and placed little ponds of golden poison around the house.

Before the trip, Peter had quit a job he hated and I'd ended a contract, both confident we'd find work when we got back. When it was clear we were stuck, we'd sunk our dwindling funds into a cheap laptop and sent messages asking if anyone knew of any work we could do remotely until travel insurance came through. No one knew of anything.

I looked through the slim pickings of job ads, trying to find anything that could be done remotely. There was nothing, but I applied for one anyway, trying to make the different time zone sound like an advantage. It was a novelty to have something to do, but it was soon impossible; I kept mistaking ants on the screen for punctuation. Some dashed up my forearms in a panic. Others fled under the keys and I imagined I was mashing them as I typed. I put the laptop next to some poison to lure them out. The pond became clogged with bodies.

'I thought they were meant to die in their nests.'

'I think these guys got greedy and drowned,' Peter said. He scooped out the ants with a spoon and topped up the liquid.

'It's not helping,' I said.

Be patient, give it a little more time, I voiced in my head a moment before Peter said it. It was a long time since I'd felt surprised in a good way.

One morning in the jungle, our guide had paddled us out in a kayak to see pink river dolphins. They sounded unlikely, like a child's invention. But a pod swam next to us, skimming over and under the water, looking just like ocean ones but with mottled blushing backs. They were rumoured to take human form and impregnate sleeping women in riverside villages.

'Maybe I'll get lucky,' I'd whispered to Peter.

For years we'd been disinclined to have children. But disinclination had wavered into ambivalence, and we'd stopped using birth control two years before, saying: if it happens, it happens. It had not happened. My doctor had given me a brochure for a fertility clinic and said to think it over. This trip to child-unfriendly locations, this honeymoon we'd never taken when we got married, was meant to be us thinking about it.

On the kitchen bench an ant metropolis had formed on a sugary teaspoon. I dumped it in the sink and turned the water on hard.

Peter watched me. 'In the jungle you said you loved the ants.'

That was true. They were everywhere, walking in orderly lines with leaves hoisted overhead like parasols. 'The jungle ants, yeah. Not these arseholes.'

He cleared his throat. 'Do you think maybe you're projecting your frustration and anxiety onto them?' He said this like it might not have occurred to me.

'Really, Peter? You think?'

'Just try to chill out.'

I would have stormed out if there had been anywhere to go other than the steep rocky path in the dark. Instead I roughly turned off the tap, catching my thumbnail and tearing it painfully short in the process. A crescent of blood appeared at the ragged edge. Now look what you've made me do, I thought in general.

Later, in bed, Peter lay close on his side beside me, ran his hand along my side, up to my breast. I didn't respond and he turned onto his back.

'I get that we didn't choose this situation,' he said. 'But can you *try* to look at things positively?'

'You do know what's happening in the world, right?'

'Yeah, and isn't that more reason to be grateful? We're healthy and together in this beautiful place.'

'Beautiful?'

'It is.'

'Sorry. I'll try harder to enjoy the views.'

I rolled over, feigned sleep, lay awake for hours.

The next morning I made an effort and went with Peter on his daily walk down the path, along the beach. We were joined by the empanada dogs.

'They only show up when you're here,' Peter said.

I spent the rest of the day on the laptop, hoping for a job offer. The leading news story from home was about a woman suspected of maiming her neighbours' cats because they toileted in her garden. 'Living in fear', the headline read, above a picture of an elderly couple each holding a cat: one with a ragged ear, the other a bandaged paw.

Friends at home posted like life was normal. Friends in London posted photos of daring new haircuts done on their own with nail scissors. I liked everything.

A woman I didn't know livestreamed the final hours of her mother's life. Carers positioned a phone beside her mother's bed. Peter shook his head when he saw what I was watching but stayed quiet—probably glad I was distracted from the ants. In the mother's end stages, Peter's father video-called. Peter heard the chime before I could silence it, and reached over for the laptop.

'Can't you use your phone?' I said.

'Camera doesn't work. I won't be long.' He accepted the call. 'Hey, Dad!'

His father still insisted it was no worse than the flu. I waved hello and left Peter to it. By the time they finished talking the woman's mother was gone and her profile was flooded with sympathy messages.

'You made me miss it.'

'Oh come on. That is totally macabre.'

'That's not the point.'

'You don't even know them.'

'Not the point.'

We were interrupted by an email notification.

'Insurance company,' I said, and skim-read the message. 'Fuck. *Fuuuck.*'

'What? Good or bad?'

'They've turned us down. They say a pandemic is an act of God, meaning they don't have to pay out anything.'

'But we can't get home.'

I push the laptop towards him and he reads it.

'Can an act of God last this long?' he said. 'I thought that meant something instantaneous—getting struck by lightning or something.'

'They can be infinite, surely?'

'Fuck.'

We watched a world news roundup. It showed empty highways, empty temples, empty swimming pools. There were rumours of treatments, rumours of variants. An unkempt doctor talked about the mortuary being beyond capacity. The camera panned to a queue of people in a dusty ochre plaza and body bags in an open-backed truck.

'We stayed in that town,' Peter said softly. 'Remember? The hotel with the covers band, the monkey?'

I nodded, my throat tight.

We watched graves being dug by bulldozers.

Light reached my pillow from a chink in the curtains. I stretched, no idea what day it was.

'Remember weekends?' I said, but Peter was asleep.

Something was quivering on the bedside table. My eyes were bleary. I leaned closer. Ants, a frenzy of them, on an apple core—recognisable only from the stalk. I shoved Peter awake beside me, not caring if it hurt. It was the third time he had done this.

'Apple. Again.' I pulled the duvet off the bed as I got up and turned on the lights as I left the room.

He pulled a pillow over his head and groaned.

I used to believe it would take some huge betrayal to break us up. In the shower I thought maybe I was wrong. Maybe it will end not for one big reason, but for hundreds of little ones, crawling all over his bite marks in an apple.

I got dressed and left. Neither of us said a word.

Peter had been right about the store by the beach. The ant in a hat was the only poison they had. It was an hour's bus ride to the shops in the next, bigger town. But I wasn't ready to go back to the house and it wasn't like I had anything else to do. The empanada beach dogs waited with me at the bus stop.

A few minutes down the road the bus pulled over and soldiers boarded. Travel was permitted only for essential tasks. I didn't know whether the ant situation qualified as essential, but didn't have the language to explain it anyway. When a soldier got to me I held up my passport and touched my stomach in a way that could mean something medical. His eyes were inscrutable above his mask, but he nodded and kept going.

The bus followed the wide tidal river away from the coast to the city. A tsunami had once forced its way up the river, ripping out trees and swallowing houses miles inland. A wall of water—that I could accept being called an act of God.

Off the bus, I felt giddy to be out on my own, like a teenager sneaking out at night.

Food shopping was allowed and the markets were open. Fishmongers' stalls backed onto the river. They threw guts into the water for sea lions, which then heaved themselves up onto a crowded raft to take in the sun. The raft tilted wildly. The sea lions threw back their heads and jutted their throats when another encroached.

The previous week, when we'd passed through, Peter and I had stood watching from the same spot.

'We should do that too,' I'd said.

'Go swimming?'

'No. This.' I'd lifted my chin and drawn back my shoulders in imitation of the sea lions. 'As a sign, when we're fucked off and sick of each other and need some space.'

'Do you have to?'

'What? I'm only being honest,' I'd said. 'A lifetime is a long time to be together.'

'Just stop.'

'Like now, for example. I know you're sick of me right now.'

He had sighed and looked away.

A dispute broke out on the raft. Two sea lions squared off, massive and bellowing. One lurched his massive weight forward and the other backed away and tumbled into the water.

A couple walked by, holding the hands of a toddler who staggered like a tiny drunk. On the count of three they swung her between them. Their timing was perfect, like each body was an extension of the other. I smiled at them, then realised that my mouth was obscured by my mask so all they could see was my staring.

The thing I missed most was being in a crowd—maybe a party, a train station, a movie theatre lobby—and meeting eyes with Peter across the room. There was a look we always gave each other. An almost eye-roll, start of a laugh, so slight that someone watching would barely notice. But it connected us, across the space, across the people.

At the market I bought some early strawberries. A peace offering. There were three kinds of ant poison in the hardware store. I bought the one with the biggest skull and crossbones.

Until then the name had seemed a misnomer, but when I got off the bus, afternoon sea fog was rolling in, dense and fast. The empanada dogs padded alongside me for a bit. By the time I was at the path up to the house, I was on my own. The fog had closed in like white darkness—I couldn't see more than a few metres ahead. Without the view I had no way of telling how high I was so just kept walking up and up the zigzagging path. It was quiet, only the sound of my feet on the stones. Noise of waves and cars long gone. It was like the fog had muffled it all.

If humans disappeared, the ants could do as they pleased without threat of poison. It wasn't impossible. If the virus kept rolling and adapting, and if the babies people planned simply didn't arrive, it could happen. The beach dogs could regain some dignity and remember how to hunt. The sea lions could spread out and sunbathe wherever they wanted, and the pink river dolphins could swim in clear water. Earthquakes could reconfigure landscapes and no one would be there to lose their house and call it a tragedy. The jungle would creep back to cover what it used to, taking in everything we have constructed and cultivated, reclaiming the beef farms and the coffee plantations and the logging operations that were eating away at it, reducing it to a theme park of rare sightings and lucky charms. It would all come back and thrum once again with life.

'Not far now,' I said out loud. I looked back at nothing. Only the slope of the path gave me a clue to the direction to take. I approached what I thought was the light of the house. I imagined Peter inside, looking out at the white, waiting for me, but all that was visible was an indistinct glow up ahead in the fog.

I walked towards it, and I could believe that it was the end, or maybe the start, of the world.

BRENT CANTWELL

the brittles

some mornings—
most mornings come July—
by the boat place,

where the frost-frayed corner of Evans Street
and Grants Road
turned our damp-ambling schoolward,

puddles formed and froze
where pieces of pathway
petered away,

where me and my brother
removed the woollen mittens our nana knitted
and smashed the ice that formed

pre-dawn in what we called the brittles,
or I did later
when I needed a metaphor for *this*:

I could not shake out the ache,
the cold hum knelling in the knuckles
of a dumb fist.

I was looking already for *another* puddle,
another mood of mud
knowing every flippant twist of dirty water

might fall again to the brittles,
to the intricate prison of noun and shape,
to the cold chance of form on a morning of glass.

The Oyster

Take it—it is the world. Its broken shell
will pinch your skin but you'll still trace
the salt-wound of its greasy crease.
What's tucked inside is an itch
these calcium ruins, this flippant crag of spat,
just cannot scratch.
That is why—with the matt-white handle
of a freezing works knife angled away
from your body—you will pop the oyster open
like a paint tin lid revealing the pale gloop

of moot and counter-moot contrived
of hot air, a warming sea and a coal economy.
You will enjoy the salt and the spit.
For you it will be a ritual and a game:
chew to the left, chew to the right,
slurp and swallow. Me?
I can bear the outer shell of rough rebuttal,
even the hinge click of a revealing year.
But don't ask me to swallow the gelatinous
boneless things that happen!

My tongue discerns no shape in a wall of fire,
in the shriek of car steel and sap.
The bitter vinegar of *Thoughts and Prayers*
can't tenderise *one billion animals*
into palatable pieces.
Denial—dunked in the soy of saying it slow—
cannot be your condiment of choice.

You can't blanch away the burnt-out car
of afterwards. Take it if you can take it—
the world is yours—

ZOË HIGGINS

Luca

I take my cousin's baby
for a walk. *Bike*, he says
and *big truck.* He says
them over, every block,
every bike and every truck.
I have been looking for
the words to lineate
a fear that wakes me
when you turn away
across the sheet
or to describe the air,
on nights the moon
is only half itself and metal
echoes down the street.
I don't have names
for states that shake me
into sleep. Borges claims
if angels did arithmetic
they'd have a symbol
for each separate number
in eternity. Luca names
his world with certainty. *Bike*,
I say, experimentally.

Pākehātanga

At the pākehātanga session I help run for the indigenous-led conference on social transformation, everything is awkward. There are too many people running the session. We're in a lecture theatre and no one can squeeze around their small tables to talk. The architecture thwarts us like a big air-conditioned metaphor.

At the end we need to sing. The room has built up nervous energy. A suggestion: 'Purea Nei'. Counter-suggestion: for this session, we shouldn't nick a Māori song. Well, what song should we sing then? Fifty people in a straggly oval on the lino look around, hoping someone else knows what to do.

Someone suggests sounding: we will stand and make sounds, sing notes, squeak, wail or grunt together and see what happens. It sounds terrible. It goes on for a long time. There is a point where it seems to be reaching towards a kind of harmony. We stop. We look around, trying to learn if we've failed at something.

SALLY J. MORGAN

Irish Goodbye

I'm prone on the couch staring at the pale vases of grief-flowers. Condolence gifts for my mother's Covid-death. The French doors are open behind me and my wife Jess sits in a sad silent reverie watching the winds moving the trees in our tiny garden. Warm New Zealand summer, turbulent air filled with birds swooping after insects around our back deck.

A few weeks ago, just before I got the bad news, I'd been sitting in that chair facing the open doors, reading intently, head down, book open. A strange draught above my head drew my gaze up and to my left.

A pīwakawaka. Dark and blurred, moving the air around my head, fluttering the pages of our books. Softly, gently. Hardly there at all. The fantail. The harbinger.

Has it come for me or for Jess?

It went no further. It stayed around my head.

It's come for me again. My heart flutters in a tiny-winged way. I give in to it. I can't fight the sorrow any more. The pīwakawaka has visited me so often through these past months. There were flocks of them on the shores of Lake Taupō just after the first lockdown. I'd never seen so many. They massed along the water; they followed every human they saw.

They've come with us all the way! Family groups laughed to one another and shrugged. *Us too! Us too!*

Two fantails chose Jess and me, dancing along the shore as though to lead us into the water. Staying with us every step. One for Jess, and another one just for me: almost tripping me up, telling me to listen. I heard her in my head, the pīwakawaka: *It will never be the same. Take care. Take care.*

*

My mother's funeral was eighteen thousand kilometres away in England. We almost missed it, rising in the middle of the night, pressing the wrong link, joining as my brother was halfway through the eulogy that I'd spent two weeks writing to sublimate my grief. My family—the older ones who had survived their brutal encounters with Covid-19, and the younger ones who had no fear of it—sat masked in socially distanced chairs. I couldn't tell who was who.

Backs of heads, flowers and a coffin.

Sitting hunched forward on my sofa in Wellington, with Jess's arm across my shoulder, I watched as my mother's body disappeared behind a silver curtain, on its way to the oven that will turn her to dust.

Jess pulled me close.

My laptop screen was too small to contain this. I closed it.

*

The last time I saw my mother alive was at a family gathering in my brother's back garden in London in July 2019. Jess took a photo from the upstairs window and my brother said, 'God, I love family get-togethers.' We looked so much younger than we do now, two years later.

There's a thing the Americans call an *Irish goodbye*. It's when you slip invisibly out of a party because you can't face the emotion of saying goodbye.

I had become invisible and left that gathering without a word.

As I glanced back, Jean, my mum, was half hidden by my brother-in-law as he helped her into the back of the car. My sister was holding her stick to let her slide in. Frail and smiling, looking around for something, waving at no one, shadow covering her face.

I turned away and she was gone.

A year later, Mum's in her house in Telford on the English/Welsh border and I'm at home in New Zealand, Skyping invisibly to her landline.

She says, 'I won't get it, or if I do, I'll survive. That Egyptian fortune-teller said I'd live to be ninety-four.' In her mind her time is set, she's practically immortal. But the story has changed. He used to say she'd reach ninety-two.

What good would it do to correct her? What would I say? *No, Mum, he said you'd die round about now.* She's a few weeks away from her ninety-second birthday.

Instead, I encourage caution. 'Just keep clear of people, okay? Stay at home, get your shopping delivered.'

My sister has already had Covid-19 and survived, but only barely. It invaded her gastric system so they didn't recognise it until she was hospitalised. My aunt and my brother would later get it in the same way. Nothing in the lungs.

Just diarrhoea. Fever. Listlessness. No appetite. Dehydration and low oxygen.

Maybe there's something genetic in us. Something that makes us get it differently from most people. Something that allows survival.

*

On Christmas day my mother goes into hospital with a urinary tract infection. My heart sinks because thirty years ago to the day, my father was wheeled into an ambulance, moaning and vomiting. My mother and I went with him, and the turkey sat uncooked on the kitchen table, a pile of sprouts half peeled.

He had vomited up his medications and was delirious.

The young doctor was draped in silver tinsel streamers and wore reindeer horns on his head. He looked confused when I told him Dad had a high-grade glioma.

'Gli-o-ma?' He practically spelled it out.

'It's a brain tumour,' I said. 'An aggressive brain tumour.'

'Oh, then we'd better keep him in.'

He never came home again.

*

In Telford Hospital, Mum recovers well and I telephone across time zones.

'Jeanette, it's your daughter,' the nurse says, and I hear the handset scuffling in the handover.

'Which one?'

'The one in New Zealand.'

'Ooh!' Her voice is shrill with delight, and I feel myself smiling.

'We're calling her the Queen,' the nurse continues before putting her on, 'because she gets so many calls, don't we, Jean?'

'Well, I am very popular.'

She's right. She is.

The day before they discharge her, she catches Covid-19 from someone on the ward. She's rushed from the hospital to a Covid Unit in a care home in the Shropshire countryside.

They don't give us a choice. By the time they tell my brother, she's already there.

'It's a lovely place,' Mum says weakly when I phone her in the middle of my night. 'I can see nice gardens through the window. Oh ...' Someone has distracted her and I hear the clinking of china, 'That's nice. They've brought me a cup of tea.'

'I'm glad they're looking after you.'

'Yes, they are.'

'I'll be over as soon as we can travel, and we'll see you then.'

'Yes, love, see you then.'

⋆

A message from my brother flashes up on my iPhone: *Ring me, Sal. It's not good.*

His voice is halting and strained, 'She's gone downhill.'

'Is it in her lungs?'

'No. Still diarrhoea and no appetite. She's sleeping all the time and they said she's getting weak from dehydration. They've got her on morphine.'

'Aren't they hydrating her?'

'They'll give her liquid if she asks for it. But she doesn't ask.'

'And she's on morphine?'

'Yes.'

There's a long silence between us, as I think about what he's saying and feel every centimetre of the eighteen thousand kilometres keeping me from her.

'Why aren't they giving her intravenous fluids?'

His breath flutters and chokes. 'They say they've got no one qualified.'

I struggle to take in what he's telling me. 'But somebody's giving her morphine,' I say. 'How can they be qualified for that, but not to put in a drip?'

What the fuck is this place they've sent her to?

'They're saying they can't do anything for her except keep her comfortable.'

I feel the weight he's carrying. We don't know it yet, but long Covid will drain both him and my sister for months to come. Questions are bouncing around my head like fireballs but I don't ask them because none of this is his fault.

Neither of us can breathe properly.

He clears his throat. 'They've told me to instruct an undertaker.'

⋆

After her death I rage.

Pure, clear, exquisite rage.

I lean my forehead against the bathroom mirror to feel its cold, and inside I rage like King fucking Lear on a lightning-blasted heath.

*

In the film called *Midsommar* two elderly people are forced to leap from a cliff because of their age. It's called senicide, the killing of our elders for the sin of being old.

Mum: in Telford you lay in that bed saying, *Thank you for the tea.*

You didn't know it, and neither did your children, but across the whole of England DNR orders had been applied to elderly Covid patients in care homes. Applied without consultation.

Do Not Resuscitate.

To them, you don't matter.

It's of no consequence to them that you live off your own savings, that you're a burden to no one, that you win crossword competitions, that you line-dance and break hearts. They don't care that your smile ensnares strangers and mesmerises elderly men on cruises who send you roses and beg for your hand in marriage. It means nothing to them that you built your life from the poverty of working-class South Wales, that you were the only person in your family's history to get a higher education. They don't give a shit that you are a member of Mensa with an IQ of 145, that your mind is as sharp as a knife, and you are beautiful. Still beautiful. They don't care that this illness is survivable if they only get water into you. They drug you unconscious and let you dehydrate to death because of your age.

You trust them.

And they kill you.

And I'm raging. Raging in my head, as I lie on the couch staring at vases of pale commiseration-flowers. Jess is sitting in silence, watching through the open French windows behind me as the wind moves the trees.

Suddenly she stands, saying, 'No. Oh no. Go back!' She stares at the air above my head, stretching out her hands as though dampening flames.

I half turn my face to see a female blackbird careering from under the sun umbrella that shades the picnic table on the deck. It bombs into the house like a bonfire-night rocket made of umber-brown feathers.

Flying straight towards the flowers on the unlit wood-burner, it veers around the black chimney flue, just avoiding all the delicate blooms of white and pink.

In some parts of the British Isles, a dark bird that enters your house is a dead soul, come back to visit and to give a message.

It banks hard to miss my face on its way out. The tips of its wings touch my hair. Out in the garden it barrels chaotically around the kōwhai tree and over the feijoa to disappear into the pōhutukawa.

It is wild and joyous like an out-of-control airplane with a novice pilot.

I'm laughing and pointing. 'It's Mum. She wanted to see her flowers.'

Jess is laughing too. 'What's her message? What's she saying?'

'She's telling me she doesn't know how to drive that bird.'

I'm laughing and I'm crying.

And I feel her in my heart.

TIM UPPERTON

The Kingdom of Suck Balls Mountain

Barry, Season 2, Episode 3

When Akhmal the inept Chechen hitman
is himself hit, and NoHo Hank
kicks his wounded arm and says,

'You suck balls!'—
which is unkind at such a time—
and Akhmal screeches in pain

and shouts, 'And you're the King
of Suck Balls Mountain!'
            —you have to wonder

about the Kingdom of Suck Balls Mountain,
and its castle near the mist-shrouded peak,
with its crenellated battlements,

from which you look out, on a fine day,
over Eat Shit Plain, bordered by the shining
Wouldn't Piss On You If You Were On Fire River.

Incompetency is the rule there
and government officials wear bright, ill-fitting
uniforms with brass buttons and truth be told

it's not so great, as kingdoms go,
but it beats the neighbouring kingdoms of Kiss My Ass
and That's Not What Your Mother Said,

and see how the sun burnishes the ripe barley
in the field! The wagons on the dusty roads
are fully laden, the mistle thrush pipes its song

from the wood, and NoHo Hank
has begun a shuffling kind of jig
and Akhmal, being Chechen and all,

can't help but get to his feet and join him,
clutching his wounded arm,
and the Kingdom of Suck Balls Mountain

is maybe not where you wanted to end up,
maybe not where you would wish to be a citizen,
but as you take Akhmal's hand tenderly,

so as not to hurt his arm, it's where you are,
everyone is somewhere,
like Akhmal, wounded and dancing.

JAMES PASLEY

First-home Buyers

'The whole city is becoming one big Wairau Park,' she said. She was right. She was being a snob, or at least trying to be a snob, but she was right.

'What's the alternative?' I asked.

She was quiet for a while, then said, 'What was here before.'

*

Towards the end we spent our weekends at open homes. While the rest of Auckland sat on motorways or watched kids from the sideline, we went looking for our future.

We started at the Bombay Hills and worked our way north. It lasted all of six months. We drove from house to house, peering through kitchens, bedrooms and bathrooms, asking agents who else was interested or what number the vendor would really accept. We had learned the capital value and listing price meant nothing, or if not nothing then merely a beacon from years gone by, years before the big boom and dusty aftermath.

'There's no magic number,' more than one agent told us, but there always was.

We usually spent our mornings at my flat, eating and drinking, scrolling through listings on Trade Me. We looked for clusters of open homes in 'affordable' suburbs like Māngere or Sunnynook, always heading a bit further north, but we never made a route or list so we often had to double back and spent longer on the roads than we should have.

Some days I got irritated by how much fuel and time we wasted, at the increased chance of a DUI. Still, we never got caught. I had been a courier for my dad for a few months (he was a genius; the guy knew the name of every street in Auckland) and had spent a couple of Valentine's Days delivering bouquets for a florist ex-girlfriend, so I knew all of the back streets, all of the connections and quiet routes.

It was only as we left the last house of the day that I really started worrying. By then the wine was fading, and if it was late and if we hadn't found 'the one'

I would get furious and shove Lucy away when she tried to get close. Then she would watch me silently drive all the way home. She knew how it unnerved me.

*

Our relationship was not perfect. There were long dull days, studying and working and quitting.

Our weekends were different but even when they started well we always had a comedown. At the time I thought that it was only natural. There was my driving: speeding down back roads, thumping over speed bumps, rolling through stop signs. Somehow we always made it and that made us feel huge. And who could forget all those first-home buyers who actually took us seriously, who looked at us with such concern? Were we the couple who were going to steal their dream this time?

We were a few years older than most, and while they were nervous to leave a good impression, we just wanted to be remembered. We did dumb stuff. If there were no parks on the road—some open homes brought desperate hordes and those hordes formed long lines—we'd drive up over the kerb and park on the grass, then walk right past the line, like we hadn't seen them. We acted like we were a threat and they believed it.

Unfortunately she did too. She thought we were really looking. I don't know if it was worse that she believed it or that I was responsible.

See, we began with a misunderstanding. I threw out a line, one of many, but this one caught and the thread pulled and lengthened, suddenly bearing an unreasonable amount of weight. On our second night together, while the TV flickered over our faces, she told me she had grown up renting, how the kitchens never had ovens or dishwashers, how that wasn't going to be her future. She said it like it meant we couldn't be together. She said it like she was looking for a provider and that provider wasn't me. Overwhelmed by a sudden need for her and her disorientating brown eyes, I said I was good for it. I told her I would be the one who would make it happen.

'How?' she asked, looking around the apartment I shared with two others. I remember the way she pushed her hair back then as if she was reassessing.

'My grandma,' I said, 'left me some money.'

I think I mentioned six figures, I don't know. I can't really remember anything except her offering to top me up for the first time that evening.

'That's so nice,' she said.

If it makes any difference, Grandma had wanted to leave me some money. She told me that much as we ate refrigerated mandarins in the hospice carpark a couple of days before she died. It was just that right after she died my grandfather remarried the big-bosomed nurse who cared for Grandma on her way out, and left everything to her.

Purchasing had never been the point. To be honest, I don't really know why we went. It almost started out as a joke, something to do on Saturday afternoons. But then we got into it. We kept going. I told myself it was to bear witness, but it wasn't that simple. What I did know, what I knew in my heart, was that we belonged with the renters and that was unlikely to change. But Lucy had got confused (I had confused her) and she thought she could swap sides. Except it didn't work that way. It hadn't for the longest time.

*

The day I'm recalling was actually a Sunday. We rarely did Sundays and as hard as I try I can't remember why we didn't go out on the Saturday; or maybe we did—maybe we were just so sick of each other we decided to spend the whole weekend driving from house to unaffordable house.

I remember she was looking unusually pale. She had olive skin but she was all washed out. I had the shakes and I remember those shakes didn't go away even after I gulped the first Bloody Mary. We lingered. We spent as long as we could at home, as if we were both hoping the other would say, 'Let's not,' but in the end routine took over.

'This one?' She said, sending me the link.

'No.'

'Or this one?'

'Hell no!'

'Fine,' she said. 'Let's not bother.'

When we got to the first house in Albany, everyone looked sceptical about something, or maybe they were just unhappy. All the couples walked slowly and shouted mournfully between rooms—'Cracks in the wall' or 'Mould in the shower'. The agent grinned and bore it but no one was comfortable.

'I don't even think it's a doer-upper,' Lucy said miserably and my heart filled with an unexpected melancholy.

At about two, we showed up at our second open home. Long Bay. We had reached the edge of the city.

It took us a few minutes to find the little grey plaster box hidden between tasteless sprawling seventies' and eighties' builds, surrounded by high fences and a dozen transplanted palm trees. The fences and trees were meant to give privacy and evoke the Pacific but all they did was make it damp and dark, closed off. It looked like one of the neighbours' outhouses or servants' quarters.

'It's worth more than a million,' I said.

To get to the front door you had to climb past a tiny standalone concrete garage.

'It's too low,' she said. Her little head of shaggy hair looked odd so far above the garage roof.

'The Demio will fit,' I said.

'Better make sure.'

We had discovered the more willing you were to do bold things, the more the agent and everyone else accepted you. By the time we had parked in the garage, confirming that in fact the Demio could fit, two other couples were waiting in idle.

'I know you guys, don't I?' the agent said after I had parked back on the road, tight against the kerb. I was admiring my park so I didn't realise at first he was talking to us.

'Don't I?' he said again.

He was standing in the doorway. He thought he was better than us.

'You were interested in Awaroa Street?'

'Hmm?' Lucy said, looking at me.

'The one in Sandringham,' I reminded her.

'That was so long ago.'

'It sold for $1.7 million,' the agent said.

He was giving me a bad vibe.

'Well, I'm going to check the garden,' I said.

I didn't see Lucy for a while. Then she was beside me, flushed. 'Why'd you leave me with him?'

'What happened?' I could tell something had by the way she was looking at me, her eyes narrowed.

'There's no dishwasher,' she said. That was the first thing she checked at every house. Her future required a powerful dishwasher or there was no future. 'I asked him about it and he got all agitated and tried to call me out. He basically called me a piece of shit, said he sees our type all the time.'

'What is our type?' I asked.

'Forget it. I just want to buy the place to make a point,' she said. She watched me when she said that and I couldn't look at her.

Two women walked past us and I said loudly to her, 'Anyway, it's a leaker.'

But it wasn't enough. She wanted to scream at me, I could tell. We'd been through this before but today I couldn't bear it. I grabbed her and pulled her towards the road. The agent watched us go.

'See you again,' he called.

Lucy yelled back, 'There's no space for a fucking dishwasher!' and his face dropped. That might have been the greatest moment we had at an open home.

⋆

Maybe if we had called it a day there, things wouldn't have ended the way they did.

Maybe we would have gone to bed and slept it off and started again the next weekend. I don't know. I think I said we should go home, order dumplings and a couple of slices of cake and watch a movie. I think she refused. But for all I know it was the other way around and she had wanted to be alone with me and I couldn't face her.

Maybe, because I had nothing left to say, I told her we had to keep going.

⋆

We pulled in at a house a few streets away after a looping detour. She was breathing normally again but I didn't feel good about our chances of saving the afternoon. We had gone a little south too and I should have known that was a bad idea.

'She did leave you that money, right?'

'What?'

'Your granny.'

It was like she had finally decided to stop pretending.

'Do you think we should try somewhere else?' I said, looking at the agency name at the bottom of the For Sale sign.

She sighed. 'Why?'

'It's the same people as the last one. He might have called them.'

But we went inside. The agent was small and blonde and looked right through me while talking on her mobile. She smiled, then pointed at a logbook. I wrote down our first names but fake last names and fake numbers. I wanted to stick close to make sure the other guy wasn't on the phone giving her a heads-up, but it sounded like she was talking her kid through an algebra problem.

Lucy disappeared. After a while I left the agent too and wandered through empty bedrooms and a cluttered kitchen until I found a conservatory out back. The sun beamed in. I lay back and stared at the back yard. The grass was freshly mown but it still looked scruffy. Everything looked scruffy to me that afternoon.

'Pretty nice, huh?' The agent said, standing at the end of the couch by my feet. She wanted me to feel bad about lying down but I refused.

'Yeah,' I said. 'And yet ...'

'It doesn't fit? It was only recently added to the house. A really sad story. A young couple bought this place a few years back. All ready to start a family but then she got cancer. At the end all she wanted was a room filled with light.'

Her delivery was all wrong but it still made me think. I felt like I understood the wife. After one of our better days we would spend the evening discussing how we would improve the house and make it ours. We would paint, remove carpets, change tiles, knock down unnecessary walls and let the light in. It was always so bafflingly obvious and yet none of the owners ever made the changes. We knew they were necessary but no one else did and so we wondered if we were special, if we could see what no one else could see.

I tried not to think about the woman with cancer who must have lain there as I lay there, basking in the sun. I was finally relaxed, for the first time all weekend. I wondered if there was a way, if a bank would somehow give us a loan. Surely, I thought. They just want your money.

Then I heard Lucy laugh and my stomach clenched. She hadn't laughed like that in weeks.

*

I found her with another couple looking at an ensuite, huddled together.

'This is ...' she said and introduced me to a young, sensitive-looking woman and a guy our age or a bit older. He was balding, small and pale, bundled in an oversized leather jacket.

They were doing what we were doing, I saw that right away, but while we looked respectable, those two flaunted their lack of means like a slap in the face.

'Hi,' I said.

'Brother,' he said.

I listened to him list all of the ways they could bargain the seller down, all of the supposed flaws. He was unbearable. He loved the sound of his own voice. I wanted to get away but Lucy was enjoying him. She had a knack for finding losers.

'There's a conservatory,' I said to Lucy.

She didn't look at me. Twenty minutes ago I'd done my very best to avoid her eyes and now it was all I wanted.

'Lucy?'

She just said, 'I'll meet you there.'

I should have stayed in that ensuite, I should have made conversation until they got bored with us, but I left them and stumbled back down the stairs.

*

When I opened my eyes again the house was quiet. I was alone in the conservatory. Clouds covered the sun, then it was bright again.

I waited a while. I watched the back yard as if she might have been nearby inspecting the lawns. Then I got sick of pretending and walked out of the house.

I was sitting in the car when the agent came over. She knocked on the window. I wound it down, expecting her to say, 'You deserve better' or 'She went that way', but all she did was hand me a flyer and say, 'Auction is this Wednesday.'

*

I expected to find them drinking at the apartment but she wasn't there. In actual fact she never came back. I waited around that night. I lay on the couch and didn't sleep and when it was Monday and I had to go to work I left the key under the mat.

A few days later, when I hadn't heard from her and I realised we had gone the length of the city and come away with nothing, I dropped her things at her mum's and wished her well. I erased my Trade Me searches and stopped going. Cold turkey. I didn't even think about it. I just stopped. Some couples go bowling or out to brunch. This was our thing and without her there was no longer any point.

Much later, when I walked past another line of hopeful buyers one day, I remembered those weekends, but they had become vague and unclear, troubling, like a humid afternoon before the clouds break. All I really remembered was her during the week while I pretended to study. I remembered how whenever she was down she used to turn on the dishwasher. It didn't matter whether it was late at night or the middle of the day, whether it was full or empty—she turned it on because it was the only thing in all of the world that could calm her down. She turned it on because it sounded like rain.

KATHRYN REEVES

Fraudster

Yes, I took the money
I spent it on total shit
and now there's a six-episode podcast about me

The worst thing about the podcast
is that everyone knows what I bought

Twelve nights with prostitutes at the Hilton, two at a time
A trampoline floor in my basement
A Dyson vacuum cleaner for every room
All the LEGO sets
A Tesla that I wrote off the first week
and all the rest

The thing people most want to know is why
The second thing people want to know is how
The third thing people want to know
is how I could sleep at night
which is really the first thing

You want to know what broke inside me
I want to know that too
And I fell asleep listening to podcasts about murderers
like we all do

Jealousy

I'm too jealous to be alive
A bright-eyed six-year-old in art class
paints a picture for her parents
I'm jealous of the art teacher, the girl
the picture, the paint,
you see I am not vibrant pigment
but a grey sun
I'm jealous of the parents, of their faces
their clothes, they know how to dress
one of 800 things I don't know how to do
I only know how to find people to be jealous of
I use the internet for it
I'm very thorough

MAGGIE STURGESS

A Good Night's Sleep

He says he never dreams. She sits on the toilet and watches a salamander crawl through a crack in the wall where it turns into a toad, then a parakeet which flies out an open window. She says: if you set the intention to dream, you will dream. She has a threesome with a handsome man and a woman with a small body who unpins her underpants to reveal a pinkish smear of jelly. *A dream journal*, she suggests. She visits a coalmine-cum-amusement park and every hour there's a show: a black slurry raining on the visitors who huddle in merry clusters under the hulking machines. One morning he remembers: his father was shot while he watched, and after, an arrow pierced him in the throat. *Wait, no,* he says, *it was a laser and I felt as though I couldn't breathe.* She smiles: finally, success.

JENNA HELLER

Hot dogs

My mother loves hot dogs.
Yankee-style buns with buttered sides.
Ketchup, mustard, sweet pickle relish.
In summer she takes me to swim practice three times a week
just to swing past Blackie's for a hot dog snack while I swim laps.
Her father says, *If you knew what was in a hot dog, you'd never eat one again.*
She chooses to never ask.

Our last meal together is two hot dogs each.
Yankee-style buns with buttered sides.
Ketchup, mustard, sweet pickle relish.
She talks me through the steps.
This is how you make the best hot dogs.
She does a little dance in her seat as she chews.

A few months later, on the other end of the phone,
far across the Pacific and all the way to the Eastern Seaboard,
my mother speaks through a wet cloth.
Her lungs.
We are talking
                        about nothing
                        about nothing important
We are saying goodbye without saying goodbye.
We are saying goodbye without knowing
we are saying goodbye.

We should have talked about hot dogs.
How to make them just right.
How to fry them in a pan,

add a line of ketchup down one side
mustard down the other
sweet pickle relish piled on top.
How when the buns are toasted just right
you get the best buttery crunch with each bite.

Honestly, I can't remember what we talked about.
Later that day, she is intubated.

These days, I eat hot dogs a few times a year:
Super Bowl Sunday, the Fourth of July, the end of a hot summer's day.
I trim the hot dog buns to make them Yankee-style
butter the sides generously, toast them in a hot pan.
Heinz ketchup, American-style yellow mustard.
I can't find a sweet pickle relish that tastes quite right
so I slow-fry onions instead. Do a little dance as I chew.

Washing

Water streams from the showerhead
like warm rain and you are cloistered
in mist, standing perfectly still, eyes
closed, letting the water rush over you
letting it drench your hair, slide over
your shoulders, run down your thighs
over your feet. Letting it run and run
racing itself down the drain. Such
speed. Such purpose. Such efficiency.
Burbling in haste to get away, break
free, escape. Go through the motions:
shampoo and massage, soap and lather,
rinse, and rinse again. Tilt your head
back and wash away a layer of yesterday,
a layer of last week, a layer of last year.
Tilt your head back and wash away
your stomach, your double stomach,
your ever-expanding slag of a stomach.
Tilt your head back and wash away
your front bottom, your minge, your
dirty snatch. Tilt your head back and
wash away your first impressions, your
fun bags, your nasty girls. Wash away
the wolf whistles and the fear of walking
alone. Wash away the need for a second
skin and false confidence, the imposter
and the dead weight of it all. Wash and
scrub and scrub and wash until you fall
apart and stream down the sides of the

tub, pool and circle the drain. Then wash
yourself down the drain and out the pipe
and into the gutter. Sweep yourself away,
away into the big blue nameless sea, or
wherever the wastewater goes, then out
to the shipping lanes, out to the taniwha's
playground, out and out and further out
still. Go way beyond the vanishing point.

ANGELA POPE

Waiting for the Next Thing

Once there was a video that went viral. You might have seen it on Twitter or Facebook. In it, a woman was screaming at a bus driver. She was holding a mannequin. The bus driver wanted the woman to pay a fare for the mannequin. The woman refused.

—She's not a real person, so I'm not paying for her, the woman said.

She moved up the bus with the mannequin to find a seat. The bus driver stood up and walked up the bus towards her.

—If you're not going to pay, I'll throw the thing off.

—Keep your distance, the woman screamed.

There was a tussle. An arm came off the mannequin.

—This is getting out of hand, another passenger said. A few people laughed but the bus driver didn't laugh and neither did the woman.

And then, I'm sure you'll remember this bit if you've seen it, a man stepped forward. His eyes were calm and kind. He stood up from his seat and went up to the pay machine and, without saying anything, used his Bee card to pay the fare. Later, someone would say that he was Bee-ing kind.

—You shouldn't have done that, the woman said. It's the principle.

The man didn't speak but went back to his seat.

The woman made a two-fingered gesture at the bus driver. The bus driver went red in the face. He looked for a moment as though he was going to hit her but that would have breached the social distancing rules and he was a stickler for rules. He was worried he may have got closer than two metres from her when he'd grabbed the mannequin. Later, he told me he had lost sleep over that. He moved away and was almost at the front of the bus when he saw the sign.

—Hang on, he said. Everyone on the bus has to wear a mask. It's THE LAW.

The calm man stood up again. He was the man that everyone would later call the Hero of the Moment. If you read all the comments on social media, you'll have seen that. He was a hero, a saviour, a kind man, a sweet man, the kind of man that women looked for when they wanted to have children. Where can I find a man like that? @quirkygirl tweeted. In heaven, hun, replied @forheavensake.

The hero pulled a mask from his pocket. He held it at arm's length towards the woman to put on the mannequin. He knew there was A TRICKY VIRUS on the loose and he didn't want to give it to anybody, and he didn't want them to give it to him.

The mask was still in its plastic packet.

—It's clean, he said. I haven't used it.

It was a surgical mask with loops of elastic that were supposed to hook over a person's ears, which was a problem since the mannequin had no ears.

—She doesn't have any ears, he said.

—All the better not to hear him with, the woman said, glaring at the bus driver.

—It's indecent, muttered the bus driver. You could at least have put clothes on her.

—Is that what this is about? the woman asked. The female body? Nudity?

—Let's all calm down a bit, eh, said the Hero of the Moment. Maybe you can tie the loops together behind her head. Which was what the woman did, and the Hero went back to his seat.

—Can we please go now? he said to the driver. And that was the only time in the whole episode that there was the tiniest sense that the Hero was getting a bit tetchy.

—She'll have to get off at the same stop as you, the bus driver shouted to the Hero, unless she gets off beforehand, in which case you've wasted your money.

The man shrugged.

The bus started up.

The woman said nothing. It was like all the anger had gone out of her and she had run out of puff. She was like a yacht on a lake when there's no wind. She was like an electric bike with a flat battery. She was like a bee that's run out of buzz, lying on someone's lawn waiting for the next thing. She slumped in her seat with the mannequin next to her. You won't have seen that bit because the teenage girl who filmed the altercation had stopped filming by then.

*

The teenage girl went back to listening to her podcast. She soothed herself with the dulcet tones of Jacke Wilson's *The History of Literature*. Life was a shitshow and she'd just proved it by filming an episode. But Jacke could make everything seem better. He was reading excerpts from *The Grapes of Wrath*. She laid her head back against the seat and looked out the window. *And her eyes were on the highway, where life whizzed by.*

The teenager rode the buses a lot because she couldn't find a job and her mum kept going on at her about getting one, which was annoying. So she got out of bed and she rode the bus in her onesie. Sometimes the bus drivers made a joke about it, but it was easy to pretend she couldn't hear them because she always had her earbuds in.

Sometimes she listened to podcasts and sometimes she listened to audio books. It was better to listen to books than read them because the words landed softly in her ears and it made her mind feel peaceful. Reading made her eyes hurt and she was worried she might need glasses, but glasses would cost a lot and her mother would complain.

This summer, her mother had said, you can go fruit picking. They don't have enough people to pick the fruit because the borders are shut and the migrants can't get in.

But the girl didn't want to pick fruit.

She listened to the story of the migrants from Oklahoma riding Highway 66 to California in their old truck, *twisting up into the mountains, crossing the Divide and down into the bright and terrible desert and across the desert to the mountains again, and into the rich California valleys ...* The migrants feeling the sway and jolt of their truck in the same way she felt the sway of the bus.

And while they looked out at the mountains in the distance and sought the cool shadows of trees in the heat of an American sun, she rode under the shadow of an overbridge. And when they joined the queues of people lining up for work, she turned her head and saw the people queued up outside Pak'nSave wearing their masks. *Men and women huddled in their houses, and they tied handkerchiefs over their noses when they went out.* It was all she could think about.

Then there was the woman with the mannequin getting onto the bus and a little gasp had left the teenage girl's mouth when she'd seen her. It was as though the woman had walked out of John Steinbeck's mannequin factory.

Then there was the man paying the fare which made the girl think of Mae in *The Grapes of Wrath* giving the children the candy, and the truck drivers leaving their nickels on the counter to pay for it.

It was all mixed up with her mother's voice in her head telling her to go across country, spend the summer in Otago under the hot sun that might as well be the Californian sun, to pick apricots that might as well be peaches. Either the world had gone mad or she had, and she couldn't decide which.

Later, the girl would discover that the woman on the bus with the mannequin was called Mae and she would be even more a-mae-zed.

*

Mae slumped in the seat with the mannequin. She had stuffed the amputated arm in the pocket of her rucksack, shoulder first so that the plastic hand was pointed straight up in the air like a sign pointing to heaven.

How do I know all this? I discovered it later after I tracked Mae and the others down. My editor didn't like the comments on social media. He wanted 'another angle', he said. Everyone's got it in for the bus driver, he said, but why was she carrying a fuckin' mannequin on the bus in the first place?

You'd be right in thinking that my editor is a misogynist. The #MeToo movement has failed to break through the armour he wears over his brain to preserve his outdated view of the world. If there is ever a way to blame a woman for anything, he will find it. Except in this case he was clever enough to ask a woman to find it for him, so people couldn't accuse him of being sexist.

I'd been disillusioned with my job for a while, but lockdown gave me the time to think on it more. I found myself researching women whose achievements had been overlooked, who sometimes found their husbands credited instead with their discoveries. I felt aggrieved for every one of them.

Take Joan Erikson, for example. You may have heard of her husband, Erik Erikson, whose psychosocial theory of development is still taught in teacher training colleges around the world. He defined life as a series of eight stages, starting at birth and moving right through to old age. Or did he? It turns out that Joan did most of the work in writing up that theory.

Joan and Erik, I thought. Almost like Gen and Eric, but not quite.

You don't have to accept what people do, but understand what leads them to do it, Joan had said. She was a wise woman.

*

They had all agreed to speak to me for the story, all except the bus driver. Perhaps he was hoping the story would disappear. The other three agreed to a socially distanced meeting. We met in a café and sat around the sides of a large table, leaving every other chair empty: the girl, the woman called Mae and the man, whose name it turned out was John.

—Whoa, said the girl.

—It's a common name, I said.

—S'pose, she said, but still.

—So what happened, I asked, after that?

—We went as far as Andy Bay, Mae said. Then John rang the bell for the next stop.

—I got off, John said, so Mae had to get off too.

—When she got off, the arm fell out of her rucksack, but she didn't notice, she was too busy giving the bus driver the finger, the girl said.

—The finger?

—Like this. The girl demonstrated.

—Ah, I said. I thought you meant she pulled a finger off the mannequin and gave it to him.

The girl laughed.

—I'm so embarrassed, said Mae. I don't normally behave like that.

I understood. I'd already heard some of her story over the phone, about the boutique fashion business on Dowling Street that she'd had to close. About the four employees she'd had to lay off. About how she'd sold her car in a last-ditch effort to keep it all going. About the unscrupulous landlord who'd wanted her out. About how angry she was that no one seemed to care that 90 percent of those who'd lost their jobs were women.

—Some things folk do are nice and some not so nice, said the girl. That's what John said.

—No I didn't, said John.

—John Steinbeck, said the girl.

—Who are you? Mae asked her. You never told us your name.

—I'm Anonymous because I don't want my mum to find out.

—You followed me, and I followed John, said Mae.

—I followed her, the girl told me, because I picked up the arm when it fell out of the rucksack and I went after her.

—I was following John, said Mae, because I hadn't thanked him, but he started running and so I started running. Do you know how difficult it is to run with a mannequin?

—It's not something I've tried, I said.

—It's not easy, said Mae, and she laughed. She looked surprised, like it was something her face hadn't done in a long time.

A mist hung over the still waters of the Andersons Bay inlet. John hadn't noticed Mae and the girl following him. They were hidden in the haze.

—There was a child sitting on a swing in the playground as I went past, said John. The child started to cry and I thought it was because I'd given him a fright, coming out of the mist like that. But then a dog came running across the park, racing towards us, and the mother told me the child was frightened of dogs.

—The dog was barking at me because of the mannequin, said Mae.

—No, said the girl, it was barking because it was chasing a seagull.

—It was cold, said Mae, and I wished I'd brought a jacket with me. I was wearing one of my dresses.

—I was warm, said the girl, because I was wearing my onesie.

—I was hot, said John, because I'd been running. I stopped by the inlet to take off my coat. A spoonbill was sweeping its bill through the water, looking for fish. I remember thinking, Everything's changed and yet nothing has.

—When I caught up to John, he was standing outside the Marne Street hospital, said Mae. His grandma was inside by the window waving to him. She was wearing a pale blue dress.

—I gave Mae the arm off the mannequin, said the girl, and John's grandma laughed. I could see her through the window. She was laughing so much I thought she'd have a heart attack and it would all be my fault. My mum would be so angry if I killed someone.

—The caregivers always bring grandma to the window to see me.

—The caregiver texted him, said the girl. Tell her what the text said.

—It said, Your grandma is so happy to see you have some friends, said John.

—He must have been such a loser, said the girl, before he met us.

*

My editor was annoyed that I hadn't interviewed the bus driver. But people liked the piece so much that he allowed me to write a followup about Mae's new project, 'Don't let your colours fade'. She came up with the idea after I told her about Joan Erikson's theory.

According to Joan, life was like a woven fabric. The warp was our core, what we began life with; the weft represented all our experiences. Sometimes, when life got tough, the fabric faded, but when we regained our strength it brightened.

Mae began designing colourful clothes for people like John's grandma. They had to be isolated from the rest of us but we shouldn't allow them to fade away, she said.

This was the story I wanted to tell. It didn't matter to me that someone had been left out.

The bus driver phoned me a few days after the story went online. It had resulted in more vitriol on social media. He'd even had death threats. He'd been advised not to talk to the media, but he wanted me to hear his side of the story.

He came to see me straight off his shift driving the number 10 bus back from Shiel Hill.

—I don't feel good about what happened, he said, but you have to know why.

He told me how the worry of Covid-19 had impacted his life. But hadn't the virus affected us all? Sure, it was tough being a bus driver, but wasn't it tough being a supermarket worker, a nurse, a doctor, an airline pilot? And you didn't see them all over social media acting mean and nasty and unreasonable.

Is that it? I said.

He looked away as though he was processing his thoughts. When he spoke again, his voice was quiet.

—I had a daughter, he said. She died when she was fifteen. It was twenty years ago, but you never forget. When I saw that woman get onto the bus, I thought, Jessie's alive. Here she is, all grown up, getting on my bus. It was her dark hair and the colour of her eyes above her mask, a dark green, just like Jessie's. And then she pulls that bloody great mannequin onto the bus with her with its blank look. Lifeless. It was like God was playing a trick on me. Here was Jessie dead and alive at the same time. I couldn't stand it. I wanted them both off my bus.

He looked at me and there were tears in his eyes.

As I left, I realised I was tired of always trying to find the 'right angle' on a story. I thought of John Steinbeck's words: *Maybe all men got one big soul everybody's a part of.*

CLAIRE ORCHARD

At the Southern Regional Call Centre

There's snow falling but we are warm
in our glass, steel, ceiling tile
and carpet square box, talking
on our headsets while looking out
the window at it drifting down,
piling up on the street below,
settling on trees and lampposts,
car after car shushing thickly through it,
at least, that's the sound effect we imagine,
the double glazing preventing certainty.
When did we get so tall?
When did we first notice water birds,
so hearteningly unsinkable,
on lakes? First notice lakes? Plucked
from a scene in a film today's ducks seem,
bobbing upon a surface we can see is presently
iced over. Half a gingernut drowned
in my keep cup makes no ripples, only sinks
deep, without fuss, as joy sometimes does.

Ambition

Of all the people I want to be I most want to be
Wilson Alwyn Bentley, cloud physicist,
the first person to photograph snowflakes.
When I'm a young farmer from Jericho, Vermont,
slight, yet as strong as anyone in the district,
I'll stand at my window, watching the storm,
waiting for its passing. Then, layered
in my warmest clothes, I'll go out into the snow
to hunt. Capturing my prize, I'll work fast,
sliding it carefully onto a chilled blackboard
about one foot square, keeping my distance,
knowing a touch of breath could destroy,
knowing evaporation is a constant threat.
Back in my workroom, with the assistance
of a straw splint from my mother's broom
and a turkey feather leftover from Thanksgiving,
I'll manoeuvre the candidate into position
on its glass slide. Next, still be-mittened, and using
a system of strings and pulleys, I'll drag that icy dot
into focus, peering through my lens until satisfied
the likeness is as crisp as I can make it, whereupon
I'll expose it onto a sensitised glass plate,
in order to illuminate and hand-etch the image.
Then I'll go out and do it all over again.
My father will think the whole thing
a lot of nonsense, but I will not be told
and, loving me as he does, he will indulge me.
By the time I die, very old, having succumbed

to pneumonia, my collection will span
forty-six winters, will number in the thousands,
each a singular recording of the basic unit of snow.

CAROLINE BARRON

Remorse is Memory Awake*

'You didn't have to come if you didn't want to, Mum,' snaps Laurie, snatching the birdseed bag from my hand and marching off down the road.

'No, it's fine,' I call after her, today's dull ache of parenting deficiency arriving earlier than usual. 'I'm here, aren't I?'

She's walking her usual four steps ahead of me—a habit that arrived on her twelfth birthday, on the same day as John's insensitively timed dissolution order. Two years to the day. Just because you expect something doesn't make it less painful. I sigh and try to repel the magnetic field of my inbox, which manages to envelop me even when I'm at the park.

For these last two months under lockdown I've spent my days at the kitchen table (next to Laurie, whose neuro-diverse brain implodes each day between her fourth and fifth Zoom class) trying to *un*-organise all the corporate events I'd painstakingly organised. Unstitching time, you could call it. Clients have always hired me because of my brisk efficiency—well, I'm getting damn efficient at turning back time: deleting spreadsheet lines for venue hire and emcees, and replacing them with lines for digital platform subscriptions and ticket refunds.

Beside the creek now, beneath the damp cool of a willow, we watch eight ducklings paddle next to their mother—she's managed to keep all of them overnight.

'Good job,' I whisper, glad that someone is nailing it. I look down at my Crocs and think briefly of John and his shiny new wife, and how Laurie proudly reported after her first time staying at their place on Waiheke the way her stepmother had rocked a beaded kaftan on the school run.

Laurie's handful of seeds spritzes the water's surface like spring rain. The mother duck quacks and my hearing suddenly sharpens—over in the cricket nets, the whack of bat on ball explodes like a gunshot.

'Look, little Gingey is spooked,' says Laurie. 'Something's wrong.'

She's right. The duckling, named for being a shade more auburn than its golden siblings, appears to be caught on a weed, or maybe in a current. But the water is still. I scan the creek, along the line of impressive houses that edge the park. The only sign of danger is a bag-of-bones pūkeko promenading towards us, but it soon veers off up the bank.

The mother duck quacks loudly and the next part happens in slow motion. I would give anything at all to wrest time to a complete stop so that I could do something—maybe dive in and grab the damn thing, or put my hands over my daughter's eyes to stop her seeing, for what happens next is an image no young girl needs living inside her head.

Gingey yanks downward before popping back up, cheeping like mad, then dips under again. This time we see the cause—not a weed or a current but a black slink of an eel with the duckling's webbed foot in its jaws. The mother duck darts over. Laurie pelts the eel with seeds. I stand there, frozen, marvelling at my daughter's quick thinking but not doing a damn thing.

It's too late. That little duckling, which Laurie has fed at morning tea every single day since it was born a week ago, is dragged—its glassy wee eyes terrified—beneath the surface.

That night, after a desperate day of crying on the couch, Netflix, and attempts to reassure Laurie's fixating brain that the bag of stones we collected *will* be enough for next time, I tuck her in (four times) and go to bed myself. As mothers do, I lie there, trawling through my inadequate responses to the day's events.

Then, the strangest thing happens. Suddenly, with no warning, a wall in my mind slides sideways and I'm thrown back in time to 1986, and over 100 kilometres of brilliant blue ocean to the tiny beach settlement of Awana on Aotea, Great Barrier Island. I was a year younger than Laurie is now and sporting the remains of a truly regrettable spiral perm. Bananarama was on repeat on the Walkman.

My best friend Tania and her family had taken me away on holiday with them. An antidote to the big smoke of Auckland, her dad said. We camped by a clear stream, dug a longdrop, and banged together a makeshift toilet seat from mānuka. There was a special tent where we kept the food in chillybins filled with ice, on a table made from fossicked branches we'd lashed together with flax. Her dad cooled his beers in the stream, anchored by rocks.

In the afternoons, when our salty skin had had enough sun and ocean for the day, we'd retreat into our pup-tent and read, or write stories in the notebook I'd packed. There's a photo of us doing that very thing—me with a pen poised above the paper, Tania leaning in with a new idea to add. Two books are laid open, face down, on our sleeping bags. I know what one of them is: *The Neverending Story* was in my Christmas stocking that year, and I was obsessed with the book and the film: a boy escapes real life by hiding in a dusty school attic where the magical book sucks him through its pages into an enchanted world, where he battles evil and transforms into a hero. I've still got that book. Spine cracked. *Sarah McDonald* scrawled on the inside cover, along with a landline number so short it reveals my age.

I didn't realise at the time but of course the stories we wrote that summer were about two young girls bored with their suburban lives, transported into a magical realm where the creatures and characters of that world recognised something in them—bravery, royalty, leadership—that the children might have seen themselves if only they'd looked more closely.

If I dip back into the memory I can see a pile of shells on each of our sleeping bags. It's hard to make out what each one is but I'm sure there would be cat's eyes and morning stars, an ostrich foot, ring shells, hinged pipi like butterfly wings, and maybe one fluted scallop shell (a.k.a. Dad's ashtray) for them all to nestle in. These shells would have joined the others I had at home on my bookshelf, each with three names—common name, scientific name and Māori name—written on narrow labels cut from an old exercise book, with a pale blue line visible at the top and bottom where I hadn't quite cut straight.

I think about that now, and what Mum always said about being careful to use the right words to name things, and I know that I'd been over-cautious as a kid—naming those shells in every possible way to make sure I kept everyone happy.

Just then, another memory intrudes. It's from just before the breakup, more than two years ago, and it's of John and me in the kitchen. I'm in the process of restacking the dishwasher because he's done it wrong.

'You've got to loosen up, babe,' he says, laughing. 'Rules are made to be broken.'

He certainly followed his own advice—less than a month after that he broke every one of our marriage vows to be with *her*. Eleven years down the toilet, just like that. I close my eyes and slide the memory away. That's not a rabbit hole for tonight.

Anyway, one twilight on the Barrier trip we followed the stream across the field towards the ocean, with some leftover sausages in a bread bag for bait and a couple of handlines. I'd never been eeling before. Tania's dad showed me how to unspool my line, plinking it into the water and waiting for a bite. It was different somehow to the rod fishing I'd done with Dad on the jetty at Okahu Bay, hats pulled down low over our eyes, cars streaming past on the road behind us. Eeling was grimier. More primal.

As I lie here in bed tonight, thirty-five years later, the present continues to reel out of control, like falling backwards over a step you don't realise is there. It's as though I've entered some peculiar new relationship with time and memory, with eels being a bizarre common factor. I don't know why I am back there at Great Barrier, or what the past is trying to whisper to me. The only way to understand is to go back there, so I close my eyes and sink beneath.

I was the only one to catch anything that night—a terrifying eel that corkscrewed its way up the line towards my hands. I squealed and dropped the whole thing, but Tania's dad was quick enough to snatch up the handle, just as the eel snaked towards the water, line trailing behind it.

That was when I realised I was completely out of my depth: that Tania's family lived entirely differently to mine. We were campgrounders—$18 per night, ablution block included, content with the sounds of other families on all sides. Tania's family were solitary campers—at home in the wilderness, unafraid. They understood some kind of outdoor code I did not.

Tania's dad wrested the writhing eel onto the grass—an ancient monster, it seemed, from the bowels of the earth—and then whacked its head off with the machete he'd carried slung over his back. I screamed as the head sprang away from the body, landing a full metre away. Tania's brother Ryan cracked up. We stood there, Tania's face flushed with the yellow light of the torch she held.

'Hold the light steady,' her dad said.

With one hand on the eel's tail and the other on the severed end, he slipped the knife in and tugged it down the length of its body, the sound like Velcro ripping apart. The image I see now is from that moment when the two halves fell away from each other and the bloody tangle of guts slid out. But no, here's another memory that superimposes the last. What I remember now is this: inside the eel was a trio of hairless baby bunnies, perfectly formed. Undigested. I swallowed the sour bile springing into my throat and kept my torch beam fixed on the bunnies. No movement. I knew that Tania was watching me in the dark to see if I was okay.

Later that night, when we'd got into our nighties and zipped up the pup-tent, we lay in our sleeping bags in the musty warmth and spoke in whispers.

'How did it get the bunnies?' I said.

Tania paused.

'Maybe the mother bunny dug its burrow too close to the edge of the creek?' she said.

I considered that and thought she might be right.

'Do you think they were alive in its stomach?' she said, our faces close together.

I thought about that for a minute, imagined myself being swallowed down whole and alive by something twenty times bigger than me.

'Maybe at first,' I said, wriggling down into my sleeping bag. 'But it'd be wet down there, wouldn't it?'

Tania sat up a little, leaning on a forearm. 'You think they might have drowned?'

She was so close I could see the fear on her face reflecting my own, even in the dark.

'I've heard drowning isn't the worst way to die,' I said. 'It's just like drifting off to sleep.'

Tania nodded, then settled back down, and I heard the rustling sound of her nylon sleeping bag rubbing against mine.

'I s'pose,' she said.

We lay there in the dark, unable to sleep, the image of that trio of babies a ghostly spectre hovering above us.

Tonight, too, I lie awake for hours. I keep challenging the memory, prodding it, to see if it will yield a little more. But most of all, I wonder how a memory as intricate as this could have resided inside me all these years, without ever surfacing, and why. I suspect it has something to do with this endless lockdown and the feeling I get every morning as I make my coffee:

that I'm living in some kind of *Truman Show* false reality in which time plays tricks on me—cards reshuffled and dealt at whim.

My mind now moves to a recent memory from four months ago. I'm at a tasting session at the Stamford Plaza to select the canapes for the climate change fundraiser I was managing. There are plates of crostini, arancini, mini-quiches and more. I tasted them all.

Yesterday, I'd had to undo all that hard work. I cancelled the venue and all those delicious canapes, and instead launched a Givealittle page and commissioned a series of thought leadership pieces—no match for the tens of thousands of dollars that the event would have raised. If only undoing climate change, or a marriage breakup, was as easy as undoing an event.

Time backs up again—I feel giddy now—to five years ago. John and I are on barstools at the kitchen island, loved-up and tipsy, arguing over ducks. I was calling him a hypocrite because he'd professed to have had a childhood pet duck named Jemima, and yet every year, on the second weekend of May, he'd go duck shooting at a mate's farm in Hunterville.

'That's why you love me,' he was saying. 'Because I know that things aren't always black and white. That two things can be true at once.'

The words 'unlike you' dangle from the end of his sentence.

Even now, some mornings when I wake, I forget that he's left me. I roll over to seek out his blue eyes, only to be felled all over again by his absence. Oh, John, I do know that two things can be true at once.

When my daughter slips into bed beside me, the clock reads 1.47am. I need her as much as she needs me.

'I can't sleep,' she says.

'Neither.'

'I miss Dad.'

My breath jags inwards. 'It's okay to miss him.'

'Do you think I'll be able to stay with them on Waiheke when lockdown's over?'

'I think so,' I say, a bolt of worry striking my chest. How will she fare there, this only child of mine, in a houseful of *her* three young children, and with all those sharp-edged Scandi chairs and macramé plant holders?

We lie there for a while longer, my fingers smoothing the delicate skin on her inside forearm.

'The eel,' she whispers.

Darkness crackles between us, and her breath has the faint tang of toothpaste. I know now that Laurie's eel moment will loom large in her life-movie for, as tonight's meanderings have reminded me, scenes of nature's mysterious and sometimes gruesome volition have a habit of hanging about. As does the image of a father and husband at the front door, looking back one last time before he leaves for good.

I shake off the memory. 'The eel,' I say.

'Would Gingey have been in pain, do you think?' she asks.

I pause. Smile. 'Drowning isn't painful, hon. I read somewhere that it's just like drifting off to sleep.'

Eventually, curled against each other, we must have slept.

*

The morning light wakes us through a narrow gap in the curtains.

'Morning, sweetie,' I say, checking my phone for the time. 'Lockdown day 66, would you believe?'

'It can't have been that long.'

I nod. 'Time is playing tricks on us.'

'Shall we go feed the ducklings today?'

I pause. Search her eyes. 'You sure?'

'I'm sure,' she says, sitting up. 'I'm still sad, but you can't control nature, right?'

After breakfast, down at the creek, seven ducklings have become three.

'Parenting fail, Mama,' I whisper.

Laurie clutches her bag of stones and fights back tears.

The ducklings' legs paddle, and the mother duck quacks, and maybe over there on the grassy bank baby rabbits are going about their business, and the sun dapples the creek's surface, and beneath, no doubt, an eel glides silently through the murk.

* This title is borrowed from a poem of the same name by Emily Dickinson.

CHRIS CANTILLON

Anniversary

Spring some sun the strings so light of rain
greenified the surface sphere a grow-fest
we lay in long grass our give-take hips a
welling then a shuddered seed, and, spent,
love's sleep limb in limb the dream intertwined,
next, dawn, a hawk above our tree-line a
mist in hills and forty years have passed
eyes (mine) a less blue you your leaner breast
the pulse resiled to flesh of youth
(lucky them) their seas of feelings no rest

KIM PIETERS

Vivacity

Set of eight drawings. All 2020, mixed media on paper, 225mmx320mm.

Kim Pieters' practice could be described as emergent, adaptive and nonlinear. She has a tendency to build her work—no matter what genre—around two or more distinct nuclei (e.g. image and text), using the juxtaposition of these autonomous yet resonant realms to create a disjunction. This disjunction allows us a rare opportunity as individual viewers the freedom to think and feel something new for ourselves. Inherent in this is an ethical dimension involved in the responsibilities we do or do not nurture toward the gathering of our own thought.

Pieters will often work in series, playing out a set of criteria. This collection, a group of drawings from 2020, is an example. An archive of her work, along with various contextual stuff can be found on her website kimpietersstudio.com

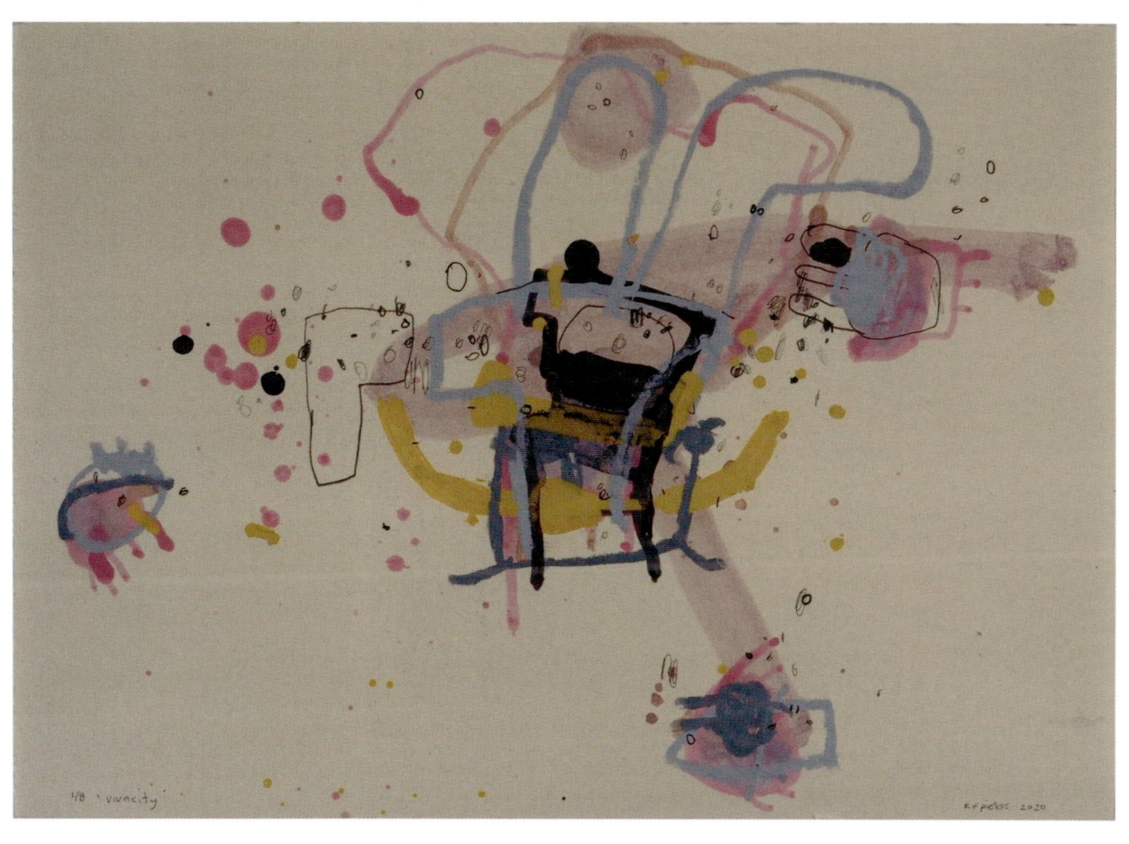
1/8 'vivacity'
kr pieters 2020

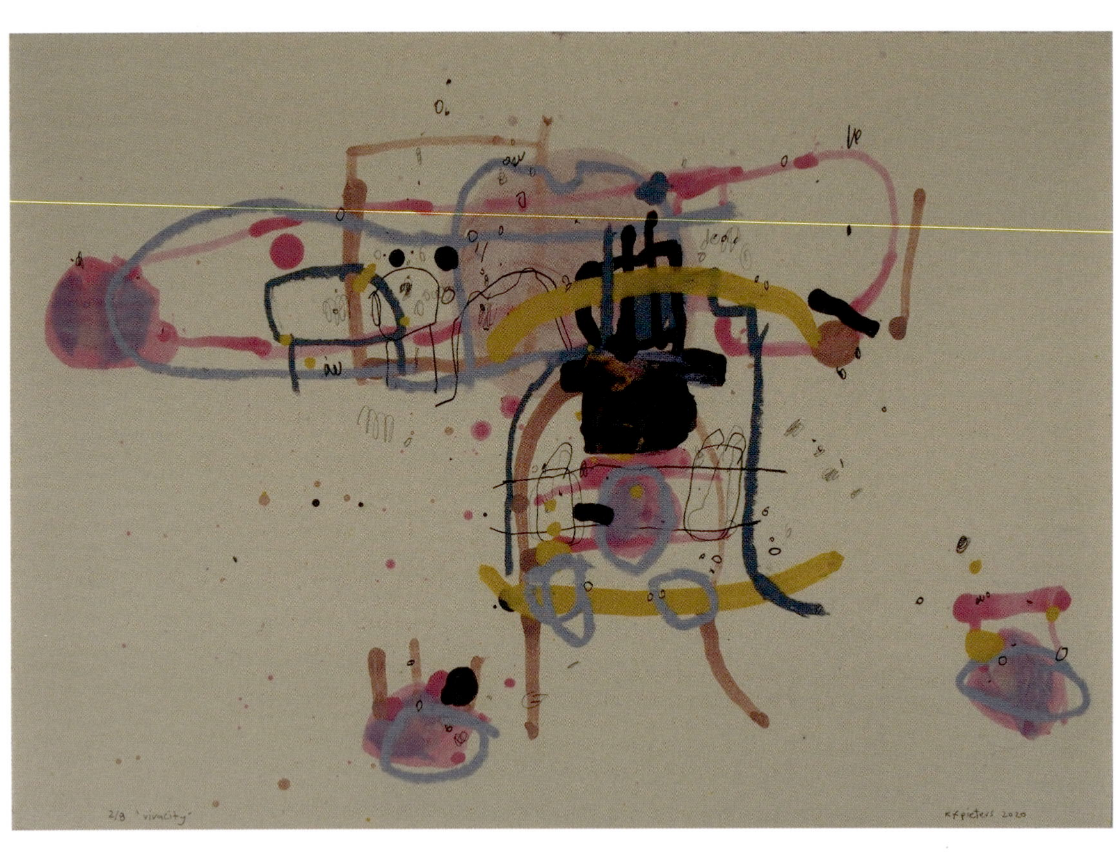
2/8 'vivacity'
kfpieters 2020

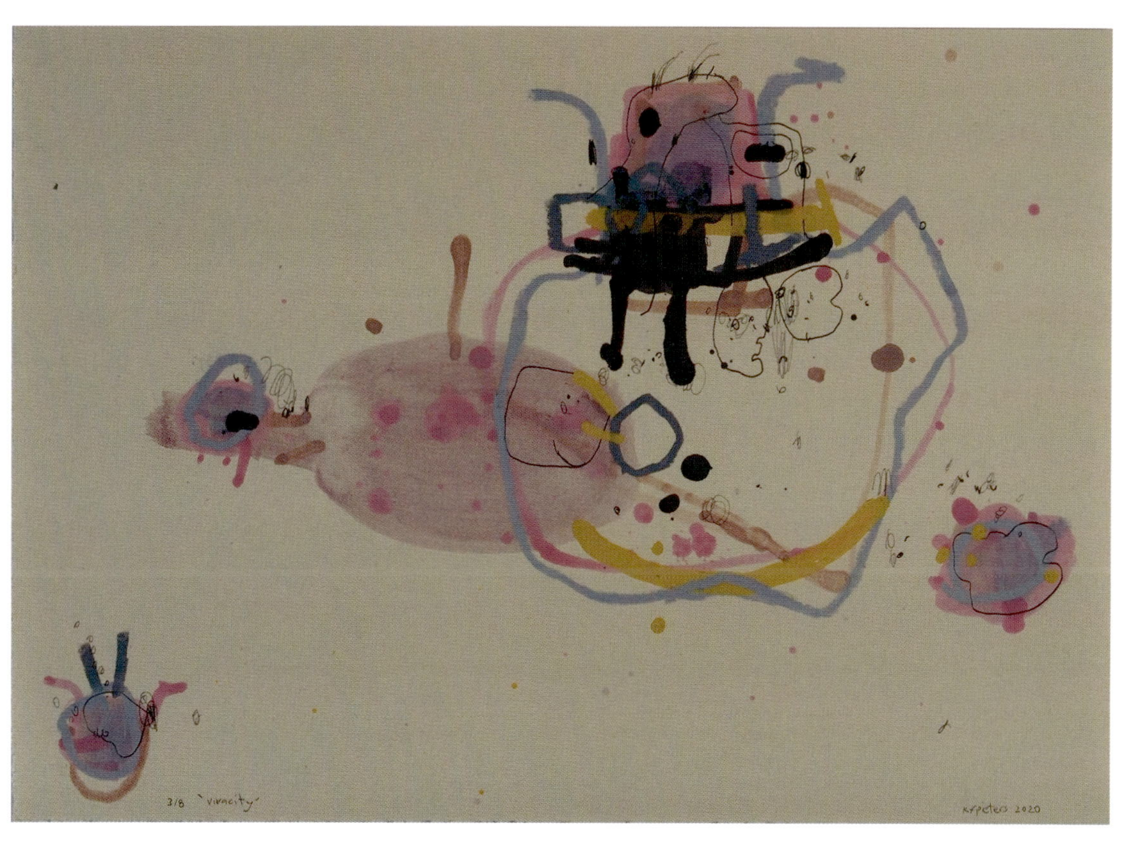
3/8 'vivacity'
krpeters 2020

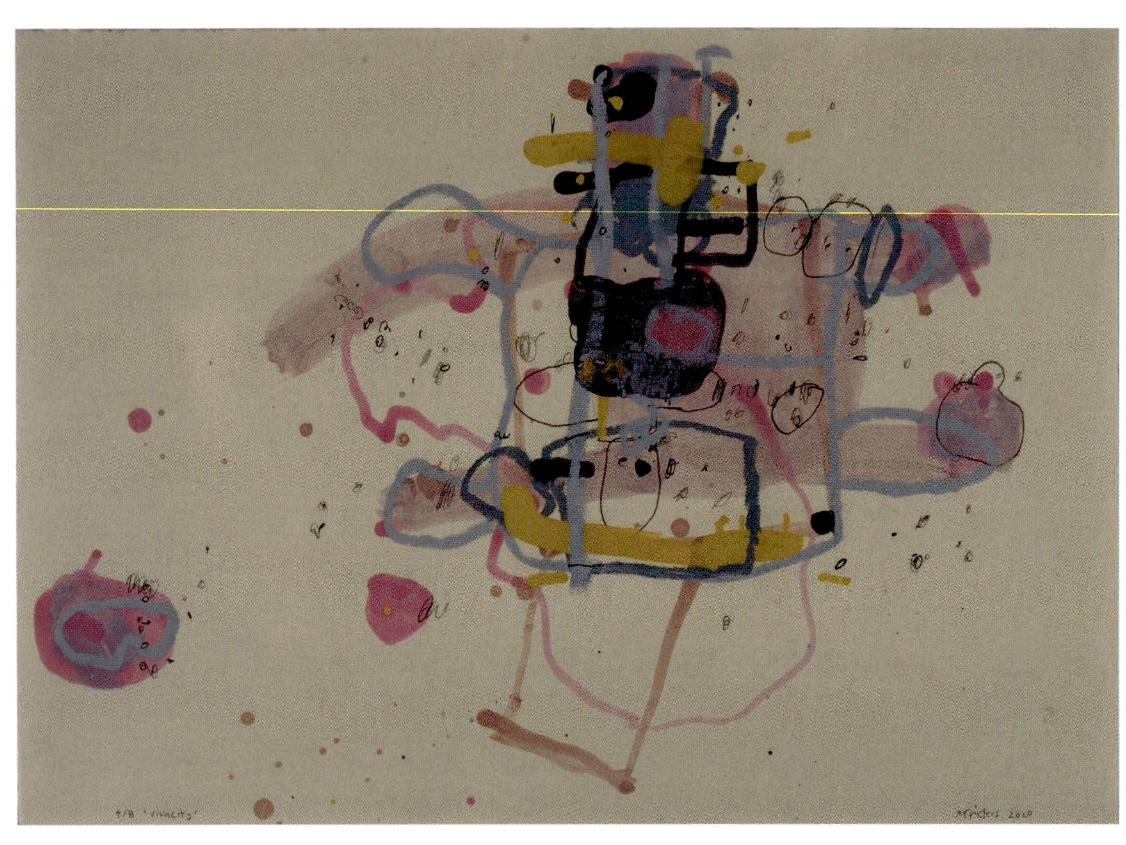
4/8 'vivacity'
KFPieters 2020

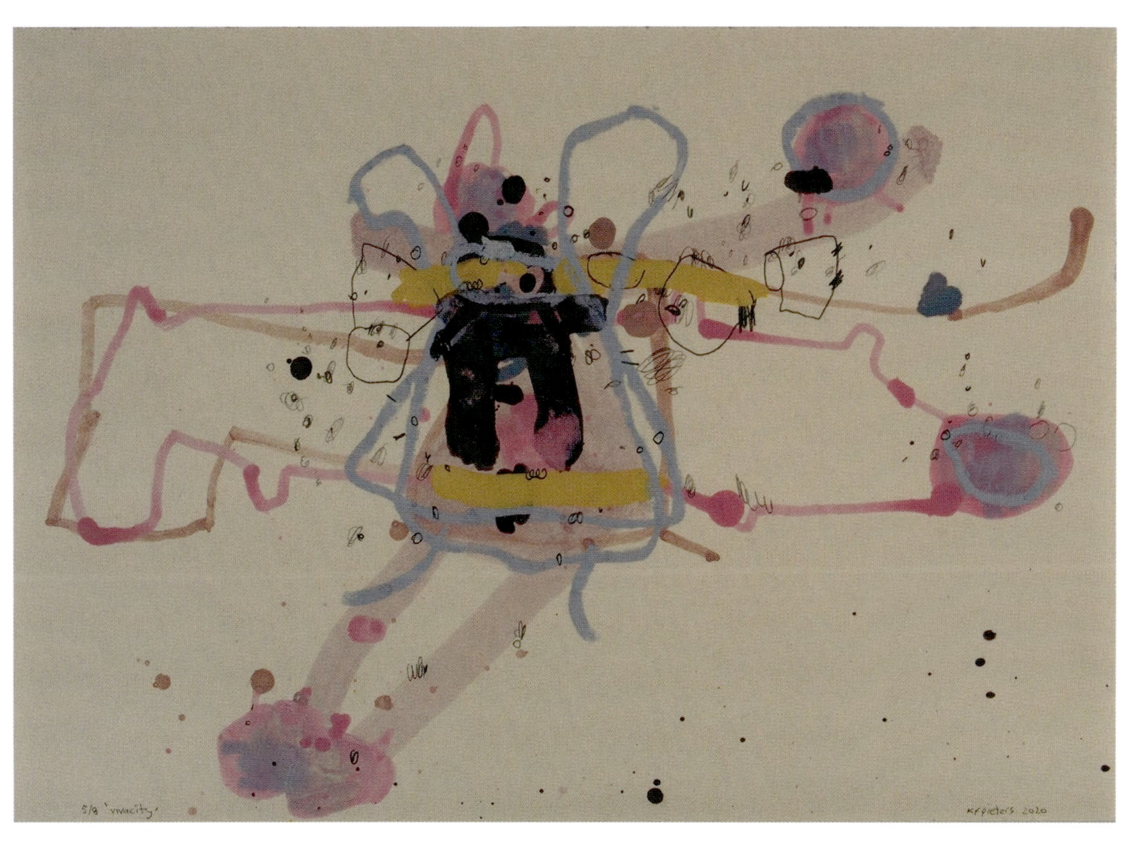
5/8 'vivacity'
kfpieters 2020

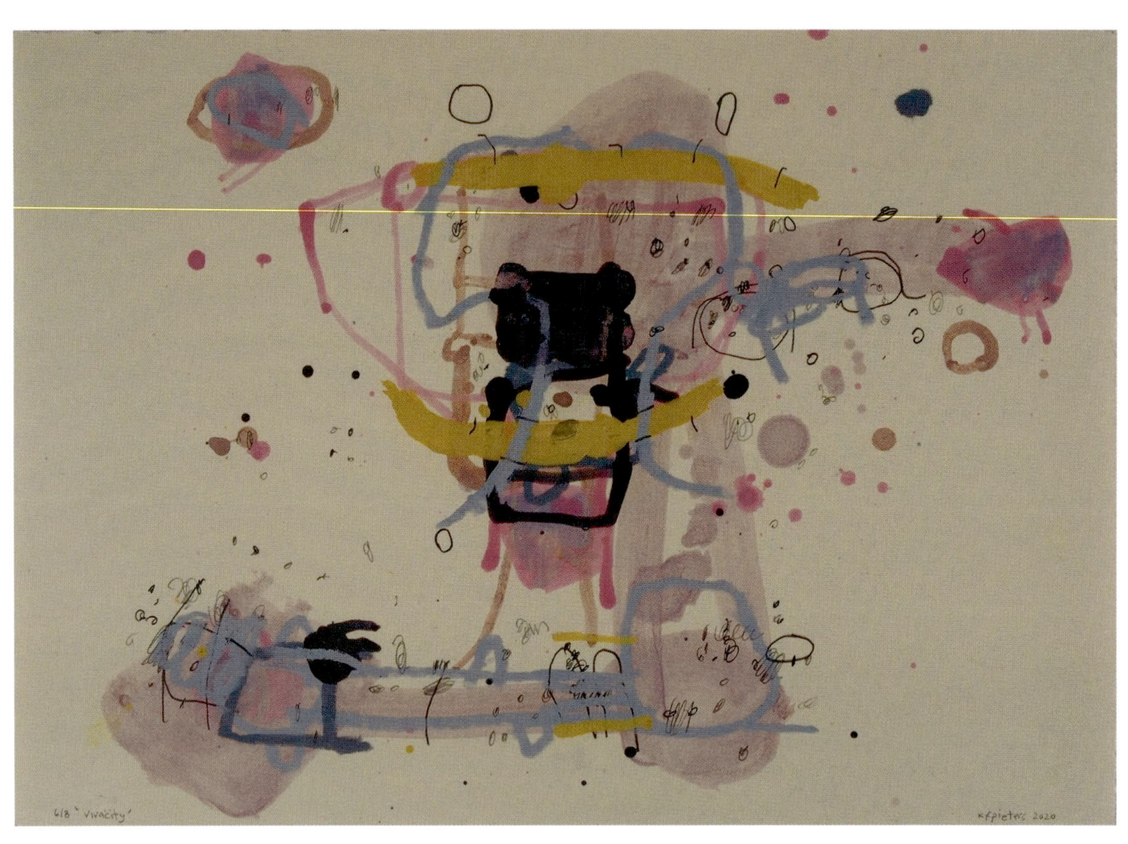
6/8 'vivacity'
kfpieters 2020

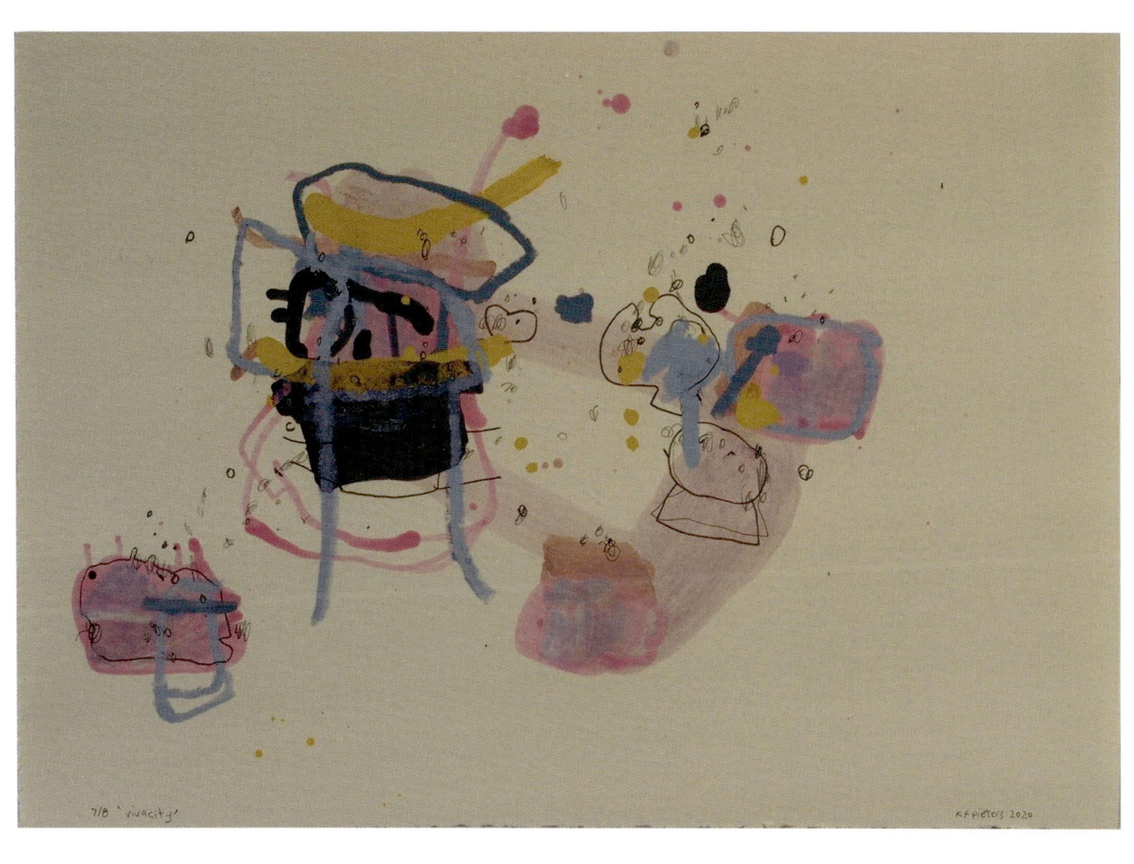
7/8 'vivacity'
KA pieters 2020

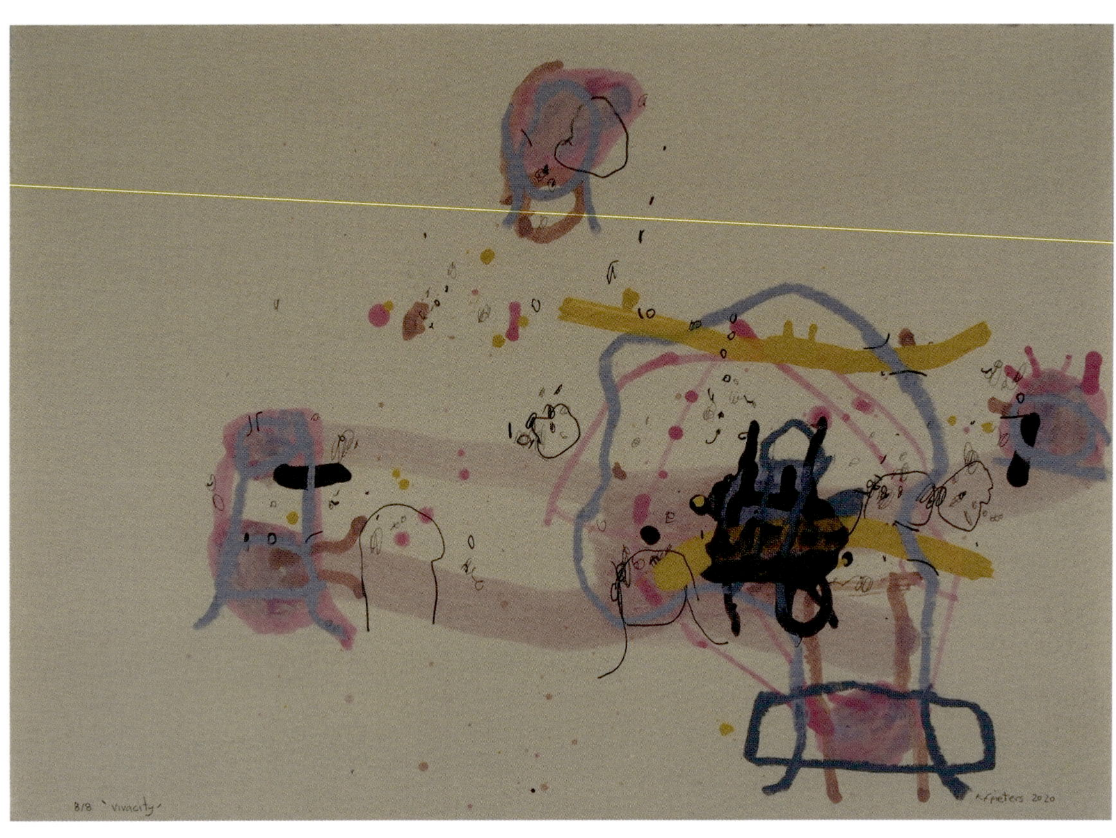
8/8 'vivacity'
peters 2020

MARGARET MOORES

Leopard Skin

(Or Cindy Sherman's Untitled Film Still #50)

Why are there three ashtrays in this picture and is it the same girl wearing leopard-skin cuffs and collar who was crying in the picture on the other page of the book? Someone has underlined *credentials* and *theatricality* and left a spiderweb of Chinese characters in the margin. The question must be one of intelligibility or a memory for back then. It is sixties décor with wooden idols and a martini glass, jazz on the turntable. Kick a shoe off and sit with one leg folded beneath you and you could be mistaken for what you want to be, except for the rest of your body which remains on high alert. There was such a thing as tear-proof mascara, and you could pull the zip as high as you wanted. You might have been better to stay blonde and to arrive much later. But for now, you are listening to angry voices in the kitchen and the sound of someone sobbing at the end of the hallway.

Yesterday's Panties

(Or Cindy Sherman's Untitled Film Still #2)

Traffic stops for blondes. A complexion so natural that you can't believe it's makeup—turning just before the shutter clicks—fingers to chin like the ads. Framed within frames, the bath towel clutched across your breasts, not slim but not fat either. Out of the picture, the shower curtain hemmed with mould, glimpse of green tiles above bath, and underfoot, a damp bathmat and yesterday's panties. You will remember this—mirror, light, click—razor knicks on your shins, getting out of the car in your too-short skirt, running barefoot up the road into the grainy half-dark at the far edge of the headlights.

JENNIFER COMPTON

My Husband Does Voiceovers

He is a voice.
He has a beautiful voice.
Sometimes I call it his chocolate voice.
Sometimes I call it The Voice of God.
Sometimes I dance around the kitchen and sing
—'We're in the money!'
        He has a top-of-the-range microphone
                in our front room.
                        When he is working he closes the door
                                but I can hear his thrilling tones
                                        reverberating throughout the house
                as he whips up interest in
                something he has no interest in.
My sister got cross with him
        because she had been bamboozled
                by the latest scare-mongering, witch-hunt thing.
        'I believed him!'—she said.
        'He's a wonderful liar,'—I replied.
I hear his voice everywhere.
        At home when I am playing click the remote,
                in a taxi with the radio on,
                        in a bus, in a shop, in a café, in a mall.
        Sometimes I am startled and blurt
        —'There's my husband!'
        And people turn and look for him.
The fact of the voice
        hanging in the air,
                and the beauty of that voice,
                        its sublime authority,

persuade us, it seems, to hardly register that
it is attached to, must be attached to, someone.
Will he say anything he is paid to say?
Yes, almost anything.
Very nearly anything.
I have asked him, when I have been intrigued
by some new story the channel is touting,
some decades-old miscarriage of justice,
some new outrage to public decency,
—'What is that all about?'
And he shrugs—'I don't know. I just say it.'
The script goes in the eyes
and out the mouth
without touching the brain.
When we met he was all for Shakespeare,
he was directing *Richard III*
and cast me as Lady Anne.
The innocent years,
when rents were cheap,
and all our friends were broke.

JOHN PRINS

But Baby, I Love You

The problem with *But Baby, I Love You* was the way Bernard Jane's publisher decided to market the collection as romantic love poems instead of what they were—an expression of Bernard's love for Sam, his first child.

When his editor suggested that the poems scanned as though they were addressing a lover, Bernard was curious, then disturbed. Sales projections confirmed it was a no-brainer. Domesticity, paternal childcare, the awe inspired by fatherhood—none of these was considered profitable in New Zealand in 1983. He would sell three times as many books filled with machismo and sexual innuendo. Bernard made the requisite subtle adjustments and approved publication. He was not proud of what he'd done, but that wasn't unusual. There was so much to be ashamed of.

An argument was building. It was Saturday and Bernard had promised to take Sam out for the day, except now Bernard had to work. Sam was crouched with his knees tucked up under his armpits. The boy had built a precarious tower of blocks, and, as with everything else, he was testing it for weaknesses and contradictions. He offered a block to Maggie.

—Mummy do?

—I'm eating my toast, darling.

Bernard crouched and added his own block to the tower. The boy snatched it, toppled the stack and demanded that Mummy do. The boy was too dependent on Maggie—she spoiled him. Poor Sam. All that would be over soon. Maggie was due any day with their second child, their restless sea-creature. Her body brimmed with the immanence of pregnancy. Maggie's bump was so pronounced that sitting on a dining chair looked uncomfortable. Even eating toast looked exhausting.

Bernard recognised Maggie's discomfort but he couldn't take Sam into a radio interview. When Bernard and Maggie started talking in the hushed tone they used before they started yelling, Sam's play lost its spontaneity. He knocked two blocks together. Exploration turned to distraction.

Bernard used his fingers to make the teabag stretch to a second cup. Maggie chewed her toast longer than necessary.

—It's okay, Sammy boy, said Bernard. We're not mad at you.

Bernard should have arranged for his mum to take Sam but he forgot, and Maggie was being unreasonable. It wasn't like she had plans. She could be intransigent in the mornings. Sam whispered incantations of nonsense, then made a low humming sound. Maggie told Bernard to keep his voice down.

—Fine, said Bernard. I'll fix it.

Sam weighed almost nothing when he clung on around Bernard's neck. Bernard slammed the door on his way out. If he could prove to Maggie how easy it was, she might take the boy out more. Sam was bored at home; they all were.

Taking a child into the city gave Bernard the same exposed sensation he felt when he wore a new style of hat, or that time he shaved off his moustache. It was impossible to know whether Sam had eaten breakfast. Everything was both 'no' and 'yes'—and 'want Mummy'. He shouldn't have yelled at Maggie. He would have to take back some of what he said.

The worst part about publishing was having to describe his work to journalists. It was the only time writing poetry felt like work. If his poems were seeds planted in the psyche of a nation, doing publicity was like helping everyone to pronounce the Latin names.

—You must be the poet, the receptionist said.

—And you must be the receptionist, said Bernard.

—Heather, she said.

Calluna vulgaris. White heather for good luck. Purple for beauty, or was it solitude? Or used as a broom, or for tea? Heather gave Bernard a white rectangular sticker with *Jane* written on it, which he slapped against his duffel coat, right where his heart was thumping away. Sam giggled in Bernard's arms while Heather played peek-a-boo behind her hands. A phone rang. Heather answered, handed Bernard a sheet of paper, hung up, excused herself and disappeared through a door behind the desk.

On the sheet was a series of rules for the studio. No swearing. Greetings occur on air, not prior. Do not touch the microphone. Relax. Please wait for Ms Carpenter to indicate that the interview has concluded; until then, it is important you assume everything is still live.

Sam knocked over an empty lampshade beside the couch. Heather reappeared, beckoning from the doorway. Sam repeated a word Bernard couldn't understand. There was no time to decipher the word. Sam said it again and again with relentless certainty. Bernard shushed him and reassured him, only half joking, that he'd get used to being misunderstood.

—Look at Heather, said Bernard. Look, she knows what I mean.

He winked at her and wrested Sam away from the couch. Heather swept through a maze of corridors smelling of fresh paint and perfume. Bernard confessed that he was a little bit nervous. She stopped, turned around and told him Gail preferred her guests to be a little bit nervous.

—But you're not going to clam up, are you Mr Jane?

—Nah nah, nothing like that.

Cables climbed and coiled like strangling vines inside the studio. Gail pointed at a pulsing red light on the wall above her and held a finger to her lips. Her hair was short and feathery. Bernard smelled incense. Sam reached for the microphone on a stand beside them. Gail widened her eyes at Heather but continued speaking with the same cool tone. Heather whisked Sam out of Bernard's arms and she was gone before either of them could protest.

Only last week, Bernard's old pal Gerald Slaney, editor of *Literally Quarterly*, fresh from a messy separation, had been stuttering and sniffing and blowing his nose ten minutes into a live interview with this woman. It had been embarrassing. Bernard wasn't exactly a stoic, but no man should be made to suffer the loss of his wife, his children and his dignity all in the same month.

Bernard liked to play these interviews with aloof ambivalence, but here, in this dimly lit wardrobe-sized room, it would be difficult to hide. He felt like he'd been invited back to Gail Carpenter's room. A window separated them from a second studio in which a round-shouldered man sat at a desk. He wore his headphones so that only one ear was covered. Sam and Heather materialised behind the man. Sam looked to be talking—actually, yelling.

Gail offered no soothing words to comfort Bernard while he balanced himself on the high stool. The timbre of her voice was smoky and crisp. She sounded youthful yet wise, an ageing male professor who'd taken in a breath of helium. The door opened behind him and he smelled Heather and coffee. She set a mug on the desk in front of him. A microphone descended from the ceiling to stop six inches from his face. The coffee was hot and bitter. Gail looked over the top of her glasses at him while she talked. He straightened his back. It was only when Gail said Bernard's name that he realised she was introducing him and they were live.

—Would you agree? said Gail.

Heather was back in the studio next door. She held Sam up to the window, and he flattened his palms and mouth on the glass.

—Sorry, said Bernard, do you mind saying that again?

—Becoming a parent, said Gail. Equal measures joy and pain?

—Oh, I don't know about equal measures, but enough pain poured in to give the drink a good kick.

—Would you mind starting by reading for us?

—Sure.

—Let's hear 'Winnicott's Decision' from your newest collection if you don't mind.

Bernard fumbled and couldn't find the page. The book dropped to the floor and he had to get down off the stool to pick it up. Gail told him it was page 27 and she padded the silence while he composed himself. She called him New Zealand's very own new romantic.

He read:

Winnicott's Decision

I cannot decide
        Made visible by the streetlight through the curtain
        In the crease of her elbow
Where I end
And you begin.

You cannot decide
        Made beautiful by the slimmest moon
A nipple disappeared, warm in the throat
Where you end
And she begins.

And you think it was you who created her
And I think it was her
And she thinks
It was you.

Bernard was not thinking about the words as he read. They were only sounds fashioned into a mask he'd made to remind himself of something he'd once read. Maggie spent so many hours on the couch, or in bed feeding Sam during those early weeks. Life's most basic authority: feed and sleep. Bernard had sat in the lounge drinking beer, writing poems, putting the kettle on.

It was a risky poem to read on national radio. A review in the *Listener* had described it as a 'transcendental memory of an orgy'. Gail called the poem smashing and sombre and dense, but not impenetrable. She smiled gently and they made eye contact for the first time. She said it felt like she was being put on, but in a pleasurable way. To Bernard's ear, the innuendo was unambiguous. Gail Carpenter was good. She had his attention.

Gail's distinguishing quality was that she didn't speak in the received pronunciation expected on the national radio station. Her elocution was nearer to that of the people Bernard kicked about with.

She was also proving more engaging and unpredictable than the usual staid formalists who asked him the questions. They covered the gentrification of Ponsonby, their favourite Gluepot gigs, Anzac Wallace's performance in *Utu*, which led to discussion of Merata Mita's new documentary, *Patu*. Bernard snarled to show Gail the tooth the cops had cracked. He'd marched towards the grunts of the brute-faced police, felt the discordant rhythm of baton-clubbed bodies, fled alongside, and comforted kids cracked open and screaming on the footpaths.

It was the last time he had felt necessary. Mita's documentary reminded everyone just how deep the cut was. Gail described in vivid detail the knot of scar tissue in Bernard's hairline where a baton thucked him after his motorbike helmet was torn off on Sandringham Road. He was proud to have been on the right side of history.

—Now Bernard, said Gail, may I ask who inspired this new collection of poems?

—Inspired, said Bernard. I'm not sure I believe in inspiration.

—Influenced, then.

She was getting close to the thing he didn't want to talk about.

—Bowie, said Bernard. I'd like to be under the influence with David Bowie.

A joke usually worked to shift the conversation.

—Uh, you're a fan?

—An admirer.

—You know, said Gail, I've been told you can learn as much about what a man's thinking by paying attention to what he *doesn't* say ...

—You mean like jazz music?

—Excuse me?

—The notes you don't play.

—You like jazz?

—I like the story of jazz.

—The point I was making—

—Look, said Bernard, if you want to know what a man's thinking, pay attention to what he's looking at.

—Except, said Gail, I work in radio.

She turned her head away from the microphone when she laughed.

—Please help me understand, she said, why your poem is named for Donald Winnicott, the child psychologist who theorised that a 'good enough' mother is what a child needs to flourish.

It had taken her a while to get here, but this, Bernard predicted, was where Gail would try to take the interview in the direction of his personal life. It would have been easier to dismiss her if he didn't like her, which was to say that it would've been easier to dismiss her if he didn't fancy her a little.

—And this from your poem 'Genealogy', Gail said: *When I look at you, I see family, In your thighs, In your cheeks, In the softness of your sleep against my chest.* It occurs to me that many of your poems could have been written to a child. Not to a lover, but to a newborn child. So I want to know why this collection is being marketed as a book of love poems and not parenthood poems?

—Parents are lovers too, said Bernard. Intermittent lovers, but—

—Please excuse my phrasing, said Gail, but I'm not buying it.

Bernard's headphones were pinching his ears against the arms of his glasses. How could love be so divisive? Love wasn't a product for sale. This was an ambush.

—Look, said Bernard, love poems are as old as language.

—Romantic love poems, you mean?

—It's not important to define love.

—But what could be more important than love?

—Context.

—And the context of these poems, said Gail, is what?

—Bloody hell.

Gail nodded almost imperceptibly and the man next door sat up straight. He adjusted his headphones to cover both ears.

—If you really want to know, Bernard said, you're right. Well done. Every word of these poems was written about my newborn son, but someone suggested, jokingly at first, that the poems scan romantically and that was how the publisher decided to market them. Sex sells, Gail. Desire pays the bills, not a father's love for his child.

—Bernard, said Gail, are you an anti-contextualist?

—Do you have children?

—No, said Gail, I'm not married.

—Well, let me tell you a secret.

—Please.

—I love my wife, but if I could only save either her or my son, I would save him every time, and so would every other father.

—As, I expect, said Gail, would every mother.

—And no one ever talks about how that feels.

—Tell me then, how does it feel?

It felt as though it was him who was being sacrificed. Restrained. Suffocated. Was that the right answer? Bernard realised he hadn't considered the logical conclusion to this idea. Emotion was not enough to sustain any sentence. The more he spoke, the further he felt from any truth.

—Ask your parents, said Bernard. They'll know.

—I'm asking you.

—Look, said Bernard, when you marry—sorry, *if* you marry—and you bring a sweet little baby into your home, that little lamb will manifest a little cloud, and it will tear you and your husband apart.

Ah damn, he'd spilt coffee on the table.

—Surely, said Gail, you don't believe this is true for every couple?

Where was the beginning of what he was saying? He had a point before he started talking; now his point was tangled up in all these uncertain words.

—It's got nothing to do with what I believe, said Bernard. It's what's happens.

—To you?

—What happens to some people.

He was hot and Gail's grin suggested he'd confirmed something she had known all along. And now he couldn't remember what he'd said. All he knew was how he felt when he said it. Hot. Angry. Frustrated.

—All I am, said Bernard, is what I can earn for my family, and I'll do whatever it takes to sell more books so I can spend more time with them, and if you think that makes me a bad person, then I'm a bad person.

—And what might the New Zealand literary scene make of your ruse to, as you say, sell more books?

—The literary scene?

—Yes, said Gail, New Zealand's writers.

—You mean those writers who finish every story at the beach, and who are unable to write a metaphor that isn't a bird or a tree or a river or a mountain, and whose self-deprecation is nothing more than thinly veiled self-loathing? That literary scene?

Many of his friends were writers, all good people, and the room had become even smaller. The incense had sucked out all the oxygen. If he had to hurt someone to escape then that's what he'd do.

—And where do you fit into this scene? said Gail.

—Look, the literary scene here is too small, too naïve, too earnest, too unsophisticated, too obsessed with identity, too immature to be anything more than ... a bunch of hobbyists who reveal their most private secrets in a desperate act of self-promotion the minute they lose faith in their work.

—They say there's no virtue in self-promotion, said Gail.

—It's true.

—Are you a difficult person?

—My wife, who, would you believe, is due with our second child, thinks so.

—Oh, congratulations.

—Thank you.

—Thank you indeed. We have been talking with Bernard Jane about his new collection of poems, *But Baby, I Love You*, published by Riparian Press.

The pips sounded for the news. The red bulb went out above Gail. Bernard waited for the signal that the mics were no longer live.

He hadn't said what he meant to say, which was that local writers were trying valiantly to articulate the question of this nation. The problem was that too many readers looked only for themselves in the writing. People weren't being taught how to read. The public were being handed portraits and they were trying to use them as mirrors.

The red light above Gail flashed like the lights of an ambulance.

—Great show, said Gail. That'll get their attention.

Bernard made sure she knew he was ignoring her.

—Oh please, Bernard, don't be upset. You'll sell your books.

Heather burst through the door.

—Mr Jane, she said, the phone's for you.

It was Maggie. The baby was coming.

Sam fell asleep on the bus ride home. Maggie was sitting up on their bed drawing long breaths. In through her nose, out through her mouth. Bernard smelled ocean salt, seaweed, and peat kicked up underfoot. The sour, fusty, sweet perfume of labour. The midwife shooed him into a corner of the room.

He felt eternal, distinct from the material of earth. The part of him that had been coaxed and protected and transformed inside Maggie was being offered back. An urge to leave rose inside of Bernard, except my God, Maggie was beautiful.

MICHAEL HARLOW

Great Men

(after Brecht)

'Great men say dumb things.'
  And then they do them.
When that plumped-up someone
  is trying to talk to you about themselves
  and they're using 'fat words' you can be
sure they are as spindle-shanked in heart
  as anyone can be. 'The dumbness of their
third-rate ideas' not even a tattered wonder.
  And you know that whenever they are
smooth-talking about peace they are preparing
  the war machine. Just to show you how dumb
they are, they keep talking to each other about
  how they are going to live forever.

MARISA CAPPETTA

Elegy for My Dad

A choir of unruly storm-wraiths rumbles in the house tonight.
Lightning-threaded clouds block the staircase
and I fear descending to the kitchen to seek water and refuge.

The spectres in Dad's house never haunt the kitchen,
it's only a room to pass through on the way to piano and guitars.
Greyhounds mill anxiously at the base of the stairs.

Heads sway, they circle, they salivate, lean skeletal bodies
entwine like eels in a basin. From the top of the stairs
I try to calm the dogs, calling to them above

the low growl of tumult that separates us.
Tomorrow the sun will banish the babel.
The dogs may still leap to their feet at the sound

of Dad's voice when the answering machine picks up calls.
I may hug his jacket close for the smell of his cologne.
We'll weave a slow reel, the dogs, the sun-chastened ghosts and me.

ERIK KENNEDY

Enclosure of the Commons II

I just want the same rights
my ancestors had:
the right to graze a space cow
or two on our common lands,

to feel a pure, almost parental joy
as they chew through neat rows
of nickel and cobalt and rhodium and gold
on a beautiful black summer's morning.

These land barons put the 'steroids'
in 'mining asteroids'.
A way of life changes so fast,
like a body in a vacuum, bursting like a berry.

Can anything really be 'owned'?
File that under *Is there such a thing as*
a stupid question? Yes, there is.
There are owners,

therefore things can be owned.
You don't get very far saying that
everything belongs to everybody.
Wake up early, strike out for your favourite spot,

and, while there's still time, make a study
of the things you love and will miss
when public access is gone: dawn light
on solar panels, the bleep-blooping of birdsong.

NATHANIEL HERZ-EDINGER

They Wander for Lack of Meat

The Irish bar on Lincoln Road was empty. Pre-Covid posters drooped from the darkened windows of its frontage—'CRAFT BEER! LIVE MUSIC FRIDAYS! $20 DRINK, BURGER 'N' CHIPS!' Alex swung the door open and slipped from daylight into a greenish haze. As his eyes adjusted, the haze sank into a cavern of varnished wood connecting the bright entrance to a yellow glow on the far wall.

The glow came from the kitchen pass, where the staff chatted—a stout Māori woman with squarely planted feet and an ironic smile, and a lanky Pākehā boy whose limbs kept crossing and uncrossing as he laughed and fidgeted. The QR code was plastered to a noticeboard that ordered Alex to 'Please SIT DOWN and let US serve YOU!!' As he tapped in his details, Alex thought about how busy the bar must have been just two days ago, the first Saturday since the end of lockdown.

At a museum in Oxford, Alex had seen a two-billion-year-old rock in a glass case with a small opening on top to let visitors touch it. Its underside was jagged and dull but the exposed patch had been worn unctuously smooth by the rubbing of millions of hands. Everything in the bar gleamed with the soft warmth of that stone—the ornately carved booths flung against the far wall; the scuffed, shining felt of the pool tables; the creaking floorboards; the copper handpulls.

Alex settled into a windowseat and peered between the posters into a slit of daylight. Across Lincoln Road people crowded outside a dairy. Only two customers were allowed in at a time and a queue spilled out of its nervously tinkling door. A woman dressed like a real estate agent came out carrying a large pack of toilet paper. She tried to hold the door open for the next in line, a portly man in a trench coat, but couldn't bear to be close to him, so she stretched herself out to hold the door with her fingertips while flattening her body against the wall.

The whole queue was stretched with this same tension, between social excitement and hygienic paranoia. A bone-thin man in a dirty woollen jumper was the only one wearing a mask. He looked scared, folding his body deep into his bubble, but when the queue moved, he inadvertently shuffled up too close to the woman in front of him. She glanced sharply over her shoulder and he held up both hands defensively, backing into the glass of the dairy and sliding away from her. Alex felt certain the man was there to buy cigarettes.

'Hey there ... what would you like?' It was the lanky Pākehā boy. Alex looked up and his heart tugged nervously to see him so close. He had a birdlike, curious face, with dark round eyes kept barely apart by a thick wedge of nose. A black nose ring and a ripe pimple had the effect of beauty spots on his otherwise clear, soft skin.

Not knowing what he wanted, Alex replied, 'You got a stout?'

'Yeah, hard.' The boy receded. Alex pulled out a faded short story collection and tried to read. He'd found it on his parents' bookshelf between Bryson and Mansfield. The stories were gruff, laconic, mysterious—like riddles. Listless men roamed the countryside, drinking, hurting each other, reminiscing. Yesterday they had fascinated Alex, but today his thoughts drifted over to the lanky boy whose calm beauty also posed itself to Alex like a riddle, while his eyes drifted to the window. A pale man in cargo shorts was pacing in front of the dairy queue, too impatient to hold his place. His T-shirt was tied like a bandanna over his face, and under the hairiness of his arms and torso lurid tattoos swum like an oil slick. In that queue—its anxiety, its chumminess, its mutual distrust—Alex saw everything he had once hated about growing up in Christchurch.

He had finished his isolation in an Auckland quarantine hotel a fortnight ago. He'd been afraid of going home. His default memory of Christchurch was of walking back from a party in the flatlands late at night. The only landmark was the glittering curve of the Port Hills against the blank sky, growing imperceptibly larger or smaller, spinning on his axis like a compass point as he wandered home half drunk and tired through the gaping monotony of the suburbs.

In that quiet, the sudden roar of a passing car was unbearably threatening. He had longed to escape—he had escaped—and now he was going back. How could there be anything left for him there when there had been nothing there in the first place? Nothing but boredom, aggression, waste. But when he finally stepped out of the airport into Christchurch's crisp autumn, and his father pulled up in a white Nissan Leaf, and they glided along the spacious stateliness of Memorial Ave to Hagley Park, where the light ran golden through the exotics, along the dumpy, sluggish Avon, then into Linwood with its sad jumble of shops, and finally through the sea-cabbage fug of the estuary's low tide—the city felt as fresh and anonymous as an unvisited European capital, utterly disconnected from the barren ruins of Alex's adolescence. He felt like a tourist. The drum-tight sheets in the guest bedroom of his parents' post-quake newbuild confirmed it. He was a guest here.

The boy reappeared with a wobbling pint glass.

'What are you reading?' he asked softly as he lowered the beer onto a coaster. The collection was splayed upside down on the table.

'Frank Sargeson, short stories. D'you know him?' In the dark, shimmering mirror of the stout, Alex could see the boy's nostrils.

'Sounds kinda familiar. Yeah. I love books, eh. We did this poem by a Māori writer in English. About rain.' Alex looked openly into the boy's face. His eyes caught on the pimple above his upper lip.

The boy seemed relaxed almost to the point of vacancy, arms sticking out of his pockets, leaning slightly forward. 'What's the story about?'

It seemed odd to Alex for a teenager in Christchurch to start a conversation with a stranger about a book. But maybe it wasn't unusual at all. Maybe this feeling was his alone, and to the boy everything felt perfectly natural.

'It's about a kid who makes friends with an old man by a lake. He tells him stories about being a sailor, adventure, that sort of thing.'

'What happens?'

'Not sure yet.' Alex took a long draught of stout. His pulse quickened as he felt himself falling into the familiar European pattern of flirtation, of interrogation and veiled meaning. 'Not sure. It could go either way.'

The boy cocked his head playfully. 'What ways are those?'

'Oh, you know. With Sargeson things usually go one of two ways. I'm Alex.' The boy's name was Ben. Alex started asking questions, one after another, like his aunt used to at Christmas. Where did Ben grow up, what did he do, what did he want to do? He'd grown up in Christchurch. Apart from tramping holidays and a trip to the theme parks in Australia, he hadn't left. He was a champion fencer.

'Long arms,' he said, flapping them out on both sides. He was stranded here for what was supposed to have been a gap year in America before studying medicine at Otago. He liked pottery, and listened to audiobooks while the wheel spun—Picketty, Peterson, Eddo-Lodge, that sort of thing. He had a soft, lilting voice, and the ungendered confidence of a Steiner kid who had never played team sports. Which high school *had* Ben gone to? With disgust Alex felt the question rising in his throat—that stuffy, parochial Christchurch question no one here could escape. He held it down and let Ben talk about books.

Every so often Ben glanced expectantly at the entrance, but no one else came in. Every so often he quietened, met Alex's eyes, and smiled. Then he asked something about somewhere Alex had been. What were the clubs like in Berlin? Alex answered hurriedly. He was embarrassed by the idea that he had been anywhere or seen anything.

His two weeks in managed isolation had formed an unbridgeable break with the past. He remembered his three years in Europe with a vividness more akin to a recurring dream than to anything he had actually experienced. Whenever he talked about it, it felt like a lie. This embarrassment added to his sense that there was something special in Ben's friendliness. Was it normal for him to talk to a stranger without any need to harden or conceal himself? Had he really grown up in Christchurch? Had no one ever screamed 'Faggot!' at Ben from a passing car? Had he never felt his heart thump on a dark, flat street as he tried to ignore an approaching group of drunks, their voices juddering with violence?

It was as if Ben had never hated this place, never feared its inhabitants. In one of those lulls, meeting Alex's gaze, Ben asked where he was from. Alex hesitated.

'I'm from right here. Christchurch.' Ben blushed and they both fell silent. He glanced again at the entrance, this time with a hint of urgency.

'Oh, right, sorry, I thought you sounded like ... I dunno.' The door finally swung open and a knot of hi-vis men crowded inside. 'Enjoy your book,' Ben said as he turned away with an uncertain ripple of emotion.

The men tried to order at the bar and joked nervously when they were sent to a table. Alex wanted to watch, to see if Ben guarded his softness around them. But they picked a booth around a corner, and except for the occasional stab of laughter, he was alone again.

He tried to finish the Sargeson story. But now, and for a long time afterwards, Ben's hoarse voice as he turned away and his flushed face kept returning to Alex as a memory both embarrassing and precious.

Outside, the dairy queue was almost gone. Wind rifled through red and yellow scraps of takeaway trash and the stream of 5pm traffic was thickening. It felt like time to go but Alex sat gazing blankly out the window. That memory was a sort of accusation—he was not a tourist, he was a part of this place. But it also suggested that some fraction of the menace he had once felt here had been illusory—that in the deafening cars, the empty lots and the crowded bars of his youth there had perhaps been people watching him with kind eyes, as he had watched Ben blush and turn away. Alex's body softened slightly, he slipped the book into his pocket, finished his stout and got up.

Ben was pouring a pint from one of the copper handpulls. The thumb of his free hand was tucked limply in his pocket.

'Can I pay here?'

'Yeah, for sure. Sorry about before—I thought you were American or something. Twelve dollars.' He finished the pour and reached languidly for the eftpos machine. He kept his eyes lowered, smiling quietly, confidently.

'Make it fourteen.'

Ben laughed through his nose. 'You even tip like an American.'

The moment stretched as they waited for the payment to process. Finally Ben looked up with glinting eyes. 'So what high school did you go to?' Alex felt a rush of irritation, but just as he was about to reply Ben's smile widened, he tossed his chin up toward the ceiling and laughed loudly. It was a gleeful, unselfconscious laugh. Alex couldn't help smiling even as he winced at being wound up so easily.

'Next time I see you I won't tip.'

Ben laughed again, then ran his hand back through his hair and set another empty pint glass on the driptray.

'Hard. Seeya round.'

'Seeya.' Alex slipped out into the cooling daylight. A large man emerged from the dairy with a large bunch of straight, green bananas. A girl in a school uniform Alex recognised—maroon jersey and gingham skirt—replaced him.

Alex buttoned his coat, crossed Lincoln Road, and joined the queue.

SARAH SCOTT

American Gothic

A guy holds a pitchfork in his right hand
like the Statue of Liberty seen through a grimy glass.
I could almost trust a man
with that much dirt on his denim
and just a few headless chickens in the yard.

Beside him a woman has a cameo
of Persephone fastened to her pale neck.
She's a smokestack, a sudden door
in the meadow where all the world's flowers flutter through.

All her roads could lead to rivers but
all her rivers have been turned into roads.
Highways on a dark tunic full of stars.

ANDREA MALCOLM

Cutting through the Cemetery

At six, a friend of my father comes to visit. In the kitchen
the two men sit at the Formica table, smoking, talking,
drinking beer while I hover in the background, landing

on snatches of conversation while attending to the concerns
of a mischievous six-year-old, such as sneaking bland,
white slices from the wooden bin, moulding the bread

into balls and rolling them across the floor for the amusement
of the cat—childish pranks not worth the attention of grown
men, when wreathed in smoke, the friend turns to Dad and says,

'The whole day digging up graves. Moving coffins backwards
and forwards. Made me sick to my stomach. Bloody motorway!'
And maybe I gasp, drop the kitten to the floor because their eyes

turn, catch me framed in the doorway and I'm packed off
to bed, no words of comfort or explanation except
an understanding that it serves me right for eavesdropping,

such sentiments being the order of the day. The lid of night
is nailed shut from above. Petrified, I lie beneath my quilt
where ballerinas vault across my chest—seemingly
more alive than I.

TIM SAUNDERS

The Mountain's Memory of Snow

I like plants
but I have never hugged a tree.
Similarly
I have never hugged my father
although I like people.

I watch him sometimes
run his thumb along
firewood and the sharp
spines of sheep.

He can name miro, tōtara,
mānuka, kānuka,
kahikatea
but forgets the names
of his children.

Sometimes the sun rises
behind his peaks
and valleys.

I like mountains
but have never felt the desire
to become one,
to inscribe my name
in an arc across the sky
with each turn,
to remind myself constantly
of snow
and its absence.

I like to think
but I don't always
write things down.
Often thoughts melt
and are forgotten by morning.

The mountain has no memory
of snow.
I watch my father's reflection
in water that slips
through smooth river stones
to the ocean's wide embrace.

BEV STEVENS

Aide-memoire

'Hello Mum. It's Bev here.' My greeting on the phone is carefully phrased and articulated. Not a casual, 'Hi Mum, it's me,' any more.

I pause. Has she heard? Has she registered who it is? Perhaps I should have added 'your daughter'.

I visualise her mind as a smudged blackboard with bits partially rubbed out. Like the names of her grandchildren. She finds a way around it. 'How are your girls?' she might ask after a half hour of detailing the latest in her declining lot: chronic chest infections, increasing deafness, loss of appetite, loss of weight, partial loss of vision in her right eye.

These are the focus of this phone call too. Mum reads out the long list she's made of her ailments for the geriatrician to fix. She doesn't accept being nearly ninety, frail and failing. The downward spiral is unacceptable. She expects a cure for her discomforts and infirmities, is determined to get back to playing bowls and Rummikub. The doggedness is commendable; the lack of realism less so.

I pull on my best semblance of patience but it's a bad fit, scratchy and uncomfortable like a cheap sweater. 'Yes, that seems like everything,' I say into the phone, smothering a sigh, 'but what about the memory loss?'

That's the real reason we made the appointment with the specialist.

'I suppose so. Some days are worse than others. I'll get Trish to add it.'

Trish is my long-suffering sister. She must be visiting for the day, her efforts to reduce Mum's dependence on her by moving further away from the retirement village thwarted. Now Trish travels further and visits for longer. There are tears and tantrums when she leaves.

Mum's forgotten that the forthcoming appointment was triggered by her less-than-stellar performance in the local doctor's mini mental-state exam: What's the date? The season? Where are we? Remembering an address, drawing the time on a clock, following instructions.

Just a few weeks ago her lawyer decided she was legally competent in the morning, but not in the afternoon. Rather a fine distinction this seemed when it came to things as significant as changing a will or entrusting us with power of attorney over her property and welfare.

We're hoping the geriatrician will tell Mum that she must move, forgo independent living, accept more support. She'll grumble, but she'll listen to him.

The phone call falters on. It's like the way Mum moves now, clutching at surfaces for balance. We're starting on the back and forth of lengthy goodbyes, the trading of umpteen platitudes, when Mum asks, 'What was the thing I was going to add to the list?'

Jolted into spontaneity, I give a half laugh. 'That could be a joke!' I say.

But it wasn't. Her response is a disconcerted silence. Chastened, I soften my tone. 'It was memory loss.'

'Oh, I'll go and tell Trish to write it down straight away. G'bye,' and she rushes away, anxiety rippling down the line.

CINDY BOTHA

strip-club neon offers *Live Nudes* in gassy pink

while at the taxi-rank
a turbaned driver bows to his phone's divine light

the cubicled dark of shopfronts
accommodates various bargaining
or an unrolled blanket

café chairs / tables
are tightly
stacked like
Hanayama puzzles

but the bus terminal's lit and the late-night InterCity
disgorges passengers with a hiss and moves off
they stand
and yawn, surprised to have bags to lift

a desk-man in the hushed
hotel lobby stares at a screen, frozen
as the shop mannequins across the street
their wigs are metallic, impeccable
but they lack mouths / eyes

there's a constant flicker in the gaming arcade

and from nowhere
a woman appears at the library dropoff and deposits
into its chute the armload of books she's found
at this late hour
to be suddenly irrelevant

REBECCA HAWKES

Venus of Ōamaru

(after Vénus Restaurée, *1936, by Man Ray)*

Milk-fed flesh all limestone hewn, your curves crumbling
like stale madeira cake, although that full-cream figure speaks

to a more supple warm-bloodedness, for so few things
are more ardently mammalian than your mammaries

letting down rivulets of colostrum-yellow calcite
when the acid rain collects on a glossy weathered nipple

where, like any public artwork, your most polished parts
are the perky mounds of breasts, buttocks and bald-buffed mons pubis.

If you were a dog or a lion they would pet your nose glassy
but even if you had a face, passing hands would hardly brush your lips,

the township's conventional erotics writ in eroding fingerprints
over your torso, the pedestal you are chained to, limbless, and none suspect

the shark teeth sheltered in your left breast or the opal bivalve buried
in your spleen, or that all they own is borrowed, like your body, from the sea.

Possum-fur Nipple Warmers

(after Venus de Milo with Drawers, *1936, by Salvador Dalí)*

At the gallery, the classical beauty has been refurbished for function,
breasts excavated into drawers fitted with tufts of fluff
where the nipples or handles should jut. Don't you want to touch?

Test the machinery, a silken glide on hidden rails. The man who remixed her
says bodies are full of dreams. Especially this sort of body,
withholding her mysteries. Well now, haven't I felt a man tugging

at my breasts like stuck drawers, asking after my dreams?
Careful men, twisting at nipples like the dial to break into a hotel safe,
decoding enigmas of the muse. There is no shame in this

although as I speak, all the shame I have somehow amassed
cranks in my chest like a heavy wheel unlocking a cavernous vault.
I am a grown adult so instead of dreams my body brims with shame.

I am primed to be mortified before doing anything wrong.
Shame lingers in my centre like the murky spring yeasts
suspended in my mother's homebrew elderflower champagne.

If you jostle my bottle I will shatter from the pressure of it
and so I am a doll machine for fermenting dreams
of catastrophe. Cut off my limbs and call me a disaster Venus.

Guys and dolls, I am not against these body games, the puzzled parts. I know
there are worse things than being collaged, and seeing one's own
amputated fragments is amusing in its way. Like scraps of possum pelt

snipped up in the grandest indignity, the plush pests dying to become
novelty nipple warmers, a frippery you might brush
with a cheeky fingertip, perky on a plastic mannequin

in a souvenir shop, while asking 'who even buys this stuff?'
Perhaps if I peel off the adhesive backing and attach those tufts to my breasts
I could pull out my own drawers, sort through the shame

into piles of that which could be donated to charitable ragpickers,
and that which must simply be thrown away. I could fill my body
with something more useful than mystery or apprehension

or other people's dreams. Certain predatory libertines
could spend so much time dreaming of the body
they might forget to keep a person in it, optional as a sachet of lavender

stuffed in the corner of a delicates drawer. But I have to live here
for as long as I can, and despite all the shame
my dreams still live on in my body,

persistent as the fine grey mould that flourishes
in the corners of my bedroom drawers, unseen,
but blooming throughout the night.

BRETT REID

Chintz

At first, I thought it was a seed.
Then, a crumb from the burnt edge
of a piece of toast. Not so slowly,
an ant was carrying something
in its mouth across the green field
of our benchtop. Only when it
stopped to rest, and I bent down,
did I see. It was another creature,
alive, upside down, its too many feet
to count calling out to missing ground.
I waited and watched. Tried to read
on their faces the drama unfolding.
Instead, I lost focus and made myself
another coffee. When I looked back
they were gone. I didn't give them
a second thought until the evening
news came on. Here it is. Observed
from a great height or an armchair
printed with hollyhocks and tulips,
all struggles seem small and distant.

MOLLY CRIGHTON

Person Train

I am a person-train with stupid luggage.
I am an esoteric metaphor chugging through a Swiss field
while Maria spins and spins and the hills are alive
with the swelling noise of industrialisation
and a nuclear winter spreads like a slow grey quilt.

I am a person-train splashing through a Bavarian ravine—
massive Cheshire smile on my face, nuclear snowflakes everywhere.
The passengers huddled in my bowels are resorting to cannibalism
which acts as a thinly veiled metaphor for the class system
and saves me the hassle of paying a chef.

I wanted to explain the stupid reality of incessantly chugging forward
in a world that is inexorably ending—rainforests balding
like an Amazon CEO's head; gulls feeding their young bottlecaps.
But all this poem has done has made me wish very much
to be in a field with you. A sunlit field, wearing a dirndl,

and watch as the nuclear sky slides closed
        like a quiet eyelid.

A Sheep Cradled by its Owner, Who Sits on a Sheepskin Rug

So this is love—you, and the way I taste.
And my skin, the feel of it, the wool-cloud
hot-cheek bristles, white as sand made of mercury.

Dead skin cradles you as you cradle me.
Pet. Sweetie. Agnus Dei.
Would you do it yourself? My flesh parting like styrofoam;
a knife, a razor, a scythe,

my bleats like the sound of a sheep being flayed
because we are just sheep being flayed.

Mornings I watch the sun rise and break
into a horizon-sized sun,
spread out through the morning
illuminated flock fog-grazing.

You hold me close, cheek pressed against my face.
Your skin, too, is soft.

LUCY CHEN

Diabetes Clinic

The pregnant woman from diabetes clinic
has written me a love letter.

She unclasps her bag and places it
on the cluttered desk between us.

It is not a ballad overflowing
with poignant phrase, unearthly devotion,

it is not a riot of wild roses
or a roiling thunderstorm in May.

To be honest, it isn't even for me.

Not *really*, though when we last spoke
I looked her in the eye, in front of her husband
and straight up asked her for one.

No, before me is a page of numbers
scrawled in blue biro
on creased hospital paper.
A garden laid out in four sections
each column stanza, code and covenant.

She picks at her sleeve and apologises
for the days with missing numbers,
the double digits over the weekend,
the tomato sauce smudge down the side.

I get the feeling she has forgotten
that this is a love letter, so I remind her
that kindness to self is also kindness
towards the ones we love
and show her today's scan.

Her expression glazes over as I go on to explain
about the future risk of recurrent
gestational diabetes mellitus and the potential
long-term progression into type 2 etc ...

Her eyes are fixed on the computer screen
at the tiny rosebud, beating.

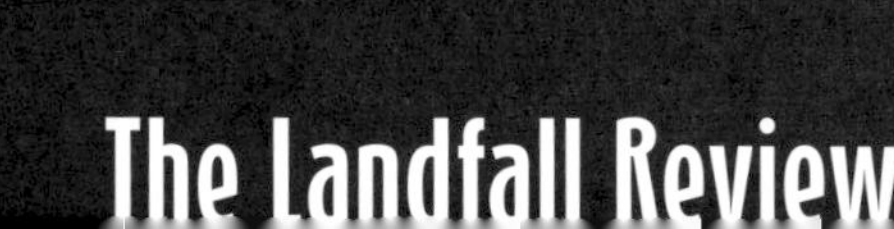
The Landfall Review

Landfall Review Online

www.landfallreview.com

Reviews posted since October 2021
(reviewer's name in brackets)

October

The Death of Music Journalism by Simon Sweetman (Tim Saunders)
Shelter by Kirsten Le Harivel (Tim Saunders)
The Oceanic Feeling by Jack Ross (Tim Saunders)
The Near Future by Hannah Watkinson (Mary Macpherson)
Conversātiō — in the company of bees by Anne Noble et al. (Mary Macpherson)
Ngā Kupu Waikato, ed. Vaughan Rapatahana (Erik Kennedy)
Take Flight, ed. Vaughan Gunson (Erik Kennedy)
Eight Poems by New Zealand Poets, 2020 with Tara McLeod (Erik Kennedy)
Strong Words #2, ed. Emma Neale (Rachel Smith)
Te Kinakina, ed. Vaughan Rapatahana (Rachel Smith)
The Impossible Resurrection of Grief by Octavia Cade (Shana Chandra)

November

The Moment, Taken by Jennifer Compton (Genevieve Scanlan)
Sleeping with Stones by Serie Barford (Genevieve Scanlan)
Rejoice Instead, ed. Pat White (Genevieve Scanlan)
The Piano Girls by Elizabeth Smither (Wendy Parkins)
Where We Swim by Ingrid Horrocks (Emma Gattey)
Kate Edger by Diana Morrow (Helen Watson White)
Fake Baby by Amy McDaid (Catherine Robertson)

December

Time to Make a Song and Dance by Murray Edmond (David Eggleton)
The Little Ache by Ian Wedde (Philip Temple)
All Tito's Children by Tim Grgec (Philip Temple)
Loop Tracks by Sue Orr (Tina Shaw)
I Wish, I Wish by Zirk van den Berg (Vaughan Rapatahana)
Ten Acceptable Acts of Arson by Jack Remiel Cottrell (Vaughan Rapatahana)
A Bathful of Kawakawa and Hot Water by Hana Pera Aoake (Angela Trolove)
Piripai by Leila Lees (Angela Trolove)
Party Legend by Sam Duckor-Jones (Angela Trolove)

February

She's a Killer by Kirsten McDougall (Wendy Parkins)
Tranquillity and Ruin by Danyl McLauchlan (Emma Gattey)
Love America by Jenny Robin Jones (Emma Gattey)
Nowhere Is Too Far Off by Peter Bland (Victor Billot)
Latitudes by Owen Leeming (Victor Billot)
After Hours Trading & The Flying Squad by Jeffrey Paparoa Holman (Victor Billot)
Times Like These by Michelle Langstone (Shana Chandra)
The Commercial Hotel by John Summers (Shana Chandra)
Unsheltered by Clare Moleta (Emma Neale)

March

Bird Collector by Alison Glenny (Emer Lyons)
The Sea Walks into a Wall by Anne Kennedy (Emer Lyons)
Sea-light by Dinah Hawken (Emer Lyons)
I Laugh Me Broken by Bridget van der Zijpp (Chris Else)
Driftdead by Mike Johnson (Chris Else)
Sparks Among the Stubble by John Weir (Genevieve Scanlan)
Meeting Rita by Jenny Powell (Genevieve Scanlan)
Locals Only by Craig Foltz (Genevieve Scanlan)
Towards Compostela by Catharina van Bohemen (Robert McLean)
Prague in My Bones by Jindra Tichy (Robert McLean)
Toto Among the Murderers by Sally Morgan (Catherine Robertson)

The Expatriate Condition

David Eggleton

Selected Poems by Harry Ricketts (Te Herenga Waka University Press, 2021), 224pp, $40

'I remember clever moody passionate girls, like Katherine Mansfield, striving to break away from the narrowness of their environment, almost nineteenth-century Russian in their yearnings, hating the traditional English Christmas in the middle of summer and the sentimental attitude towards the Mother Country. They would come to London ... exulting in their freedom, and yet keeping underneath everything their innate primness and respectability.' Thus wrote Barbara Pym in her 1958 novel *A Glass of Blessings*.

The expatriate condition is at the heart of *Selected Poems* by Harry Ricketts, while the quintessentially English novels of Barbara Pym are one of his compass points. In his poem 'Room' the poet revisits his childhood bedroom, where he 'had bronchitis and read Barbara Pym'; and in 'Lost things' he tells us, 'Evensong reminds me of Barbara Pym.' One thinks of Isaac Newton in his garden watching, as W.H. Auden says, 'the apple falling towards England': the centre of gravity.

Born in England, Ricketts emigrated to New Zealand in 1981 to take up a lectureship in the English Department at Victoria University in Wellington, and here he has remained. *Selected Poems* reveals Ricketts as an exile, taking possession of place through poems, through command of the language, finding the 'here' in elsewhere. Jet-set travel shrank the globe in the 1970s, and Ricketts made landfall in a Curnovian nation that, as Allen Curnow put it, was 'a small room with large windows', provincial to its back teeth. At the same time, he arrived just when New Zealand had left off clinging to the skirts of Mother England and was beginning to launch out more confidently, especially in the Lange years, in search of its own identity. In his poem 'A few tips for immigrants, 1981' Ricketts states:

> It is important to realise
> you're now in a Fleur Adcock poem
> in reverse ...
> you must switch off your irony, work
> on those vowels ...
> Don't you want to fit in?

The status of an expatriate, then, is that of in-betweenness. There's always a lurking awareness of a different way of doing things. Ricketts looks for parallels, echoes, harmonies, rhymes and chimes in our way of speaking—as well as dissonances. In a series of 'found sonnets' shaped out of phrases used in a Māori–English grammar book first published in Victorian times and continuously republished in the twentieth century, he reveals racial and class assumptions and biases still active in New Zealand society until recently that confirm Witi Ihimaera's experiences in his memoir *Native Son*.

Ricketts is also fascinated by the way local poets respond to literary tradition, and holds up a comical mirror to their efforts in the form of verse parodies—of

Mansfield, Curnow, Glover, Baxter, Stead, Hulme and others. He catechises the pieties of our literary nationalism with his prose poem 'Thirteen ways of starting a New Zealand novel called *Macrocarpa*': 'Hidden in the stout branches of the macrocarpa, buffeted by high winds, sat Cheryl, the rabbiter's seventh daughter, biting her knuckles.'

In the poem '14A Esmonde Road', Ricketts makes a half-sardonic pilgrimage to Frank Sargeson's place in Takapuna 'where New Zealand literature / had its origins', and claims to see a large white rabbit, Lewis Carroll-like, just slipping out of sight.

Ricketts has had a day-job as an academic, as a literary historian wrestling with the legacy of the British Empire and its post-colonial aftermath, and his poetry in a way is an adjunct to this. His sensibility is that of the administrator, or wicket-keeper, or gate-keeper, to the theme park of English literature, with its walled gardens and its side-alleys of Dickensian grotesques; its legacy of libraries where treasures of the world were brought back and transmogrified into literary artefacts by writers ranging from Samuel Butler (*Erewhon*) to Rudyard Kipling (*Kim*) to Anthony Burgess (*The Malayan Trilogy*) to John le Carré (*The Honorable Schoolboy*).

For Ricketts, poetry functions as a kind of heritage trail, steeped in classic allusions and expressed through strict verse forms. He is one attuned to England's haunted past, to the ancestral voices of ancient Albion. After such knowledge, what forgiveness? It has taken Ricketts decades to sidle in from the cold, to receive acknowledgement for his poetry from a mainstream publisher. Previously, many of his poems appeared as fugitive pieces in out-of-the-way small press publications. Perseverance, stickability, and a slowly dawning awareness from powerbrokers in the Curnovian 'small room' of the imperative of multiplicity beyond Victorian rectitude and earnestness have also served to elevate the forensic approach of Ricketts in the community discourse, to a degree.

The patchwork quilt that is *Selected Poems* comes into sharper focus when you learn that, though he was born in London and educated in the public school system and then at Oxford University, the poet spent significant periods of his childhood in Malaysia and Hong Kong, where his father was a British Army officer in the 1950s and early 1960s. In the poem 'Plunge', the poet is about to leap from a high diving board into the remembered blubbery realm of childhood anxieties in the blue depths of a swimming pool with his father looking on:

> When at last I make a decent splash,
> he's no longer around to see it.

In the many personal poems here, the emphasis is not so much on sunbeam epiphanies or youthful romantic transcendence as on wry realisations, disillusionments and rueful acknowledgements after the fact, which often sound an Audenesque note in recognition of the sheer ordinariness of our quotidian perceptions, as in the poem 'About (1980/2004/2014)':

> Old friends die; others grow devout;
> harder now to think life a gift.
> It was easy to believe and not to doubt.

Ricketts tells us that he and his father bonded most strongly over the game of cricket, and indeed Ricketts has become something of a local authority on the game, and is the author of *How to Catch a Cricket Match*. *Selected Poems* reveals his strategies to be those of a cricketer, playing the long game, slowly accumulating runs on the board, his perceptions serenely focused, his reflexes sharp. His poems are at once conversational and casual, watchful and careful.

Looking back, obsessed perhaps with the past, his love poems and poems about relationships with his student generation, slightly cryptic, clock the androgynous styles of the early 1970s and the internationalist lingua franca of the hippy counterculture, where anything beyond the pale was termed 'really weird'.

He incorporates forms as various as limericks, nonsense verse, epigrams and villanelles, but more tellingly he employs a wide range of tones to provide poems about his family—wife, sons, daughter—that are at once good-humoured and affectionate while subtly rendering a sense of confidences exchanged, secrets and intimacies confessed to, without quite going into what these might be. All is mood: we are all diminutive in our own psychodramas. And compassion is tempered by detachment, as in 'Aro Street':

> The goddess is a mess tonight.
> One lens keeps dropping from her dark
> glasses.
> Her black eye weeps for itself.

One thinks of Harold Pinter's quip that his plays are about 'the weasel under the cocktail cabinet': menace lurks within social conventions, waiting to strike the unwary.

There are some poems about Wellington's café culture—for Lauris Edmond and Bill Sewell—which are elegies, farewell salutes, poignant in the case of the early death of Sewell, co-editor with Ricketts of *New Zealand Books* in the 1990s. The poem 'For Lauris', though, is splendidly hilarious:

> 'You're someone famous, aren't you?'
> he blurted out, half-accusingly.
> 'I know, you're Janet Frame.'

Poems for absent friends, for his mother in her last days in a care home, insist on the homely, on comforting rituals based on an honest muddling through, on good manners. However, the poet is also constantly in search of the clean, clinching image that 'strikes home'. And as he puts it in 'Napier':

> The past's a mosaic so complicated only the
> foolish
> would try to simplify it ...

Napier is a word with resonance in Ricketts' vocabulary. The two great institutions of the British Empire were the army, personified in his father, and the Church of England, represented here by the novels of Barbara Pym. The placename Napier comes from a British major-general, and was intended to celebrate his 'victories' in India, an old frontier of empire. Not coincidentally, a blood-stained British army sword used in the New Zealand Wars is still on display in the Napier Museum.

The British Empire was energised by a sense of mission, a sense that it was bringing 'civilisation' to benighted lands. There's a strong whiff of 'civilisation' about *Selected Poems*, especially when the poet ventures into great art galleries—the British National Gallery, the Prado, the Getty, the Frick—and embarks on ekphrastic poems with a moralising edge that join them in spirit and purpose with the civilising mission Charles Brasch undertook in establishing *Landfall*, as Ricketts acknowledges, obliquely.

Over the course of his *Selected*, Ricketts emerges as an explorer, a surveyor, a cartographer, making 'new maps of home'—to borrow a phrase from a fellow British-New Zealand poet, Russell Haley—endeavouring to make linkages and anchoring himself in place. The cover image is a painting by Michael Hight, which, in Rickett's lexicon, stands for our post-colonial condition. A colony of brooding beehives is clustered in front of an abandoned wooden farmhouse: a ruin, a shell that has outlived its purpose.

As a poet in this ex-outpost of empire, Ricketts sees his function partly as to commemorate or rediscover what Rudyard Kipling called 'the limbo of lost endeavour', that is, the historical 'oubliette' of forgotten or neglected literary figures, standing as puzzling statues in parks, or fished out of second-hand bookshops, or retrieved in personal reminiscence. From this legion of the no-longer-read, Ricketts gathers a handful of names—Arthur Hugh Clough, Ross MacDonald, Peggy Dunstan, John Wain, George Fraser—to invoke the Judgement of History. As Ricketts tells it, we poets and writers are all such blessed fools ultimately, erratic creatures of whim and circumstance, anonymously serving in the greater cause of Literature.

Selected Poems recognises that the ghost of a quotation functions as a form of passport, and that the English language is a magic thread through the great maze of the world. It takes us from 'Elgar country' with its fox-hunting brigade—'Right on cue the Hunt clumps past'—to not meeting W.H. Auden in his carpet slippers and a jacket covered in deposits of cigarette ash; from a kind of seance with Rudyard Kipling at a literary conference in Shimla, India (in the Viceregal Lodge, 'that testament to colonial camp') to a New Zealand beach where 'the white heron does his silly walk'.

On one hand a scrap-dealer in old ironies waiting patiently for the market price to rise, on the other our deferential guide to all that's best and brightest about the expatriate state of mind, Harry Ricketts quietly smuggles in complex perception under the guise of lucid rumination and so illuminates our everywhere in a memorable and distinctive fashion.

Listening to Our Elders

Gina Cole

Haare Williams: Words of a kaumātua, edited by Witi Ihimaera (Auckland University Press, 2019), 260pp, $49.99; **Tree Sense: Ways of thinking about trees,** edited by Susette Goldsmith (Massey University Press, 2021), 256pp, $37

Two insightful books of wisdom, beauty and knowledge from the elders. The first is a collection of poetry and prose steeped in mātauranga Māori; the second is an anthology of essays, art and poetry about trees in Aotearoa. Both are well-written, engaging and compelling.

Haare Williams: Words of a kaumātua is a collection of writing introduced and edited by Witi Ihimaera, who describes Williams as 'one of our greatest elders, a singular bellbird among our native language speakers', 'the Grandfather Moses' of Māori literature and 'one of New Zealand's leading changemakers'. It is evident from Ihimaera's introduction and to all those who walk in te ao Māori that Williams is a kaumātua of great mana and knowledge, a sought-after orator, teacher and creative.

This is a beautiful collage of poetry and prose, including creative non-fiction, memoir, essays, observations, vignettes, biography, speeches, interviews, letters, historical accounts and childhood reminiscences, written in both te reo and English. The pieces weave together in surprising ways that loop back and forth along narrative lines and themes in a kaleidoscope of patterns that repeat, expand and resonate. The main feeling that struck me was of being privy to a vast treasure trove of mātauranga Māori from an esteemed kaumātua.

Williams 'grew up with his grandparents on the shores of Ōhiwa Harbour near Ōpōtiki ... within a totally Māori context, primarily Tūhoe'. His grandparents' teachings and influence are evident throughout, and they make frequent appearances in the collection.

One stunning piece of narrative is an oral transcript titled 'The Art of the Oral Storyteller'. This is a story about the kūmara—its value and importance in te ao Māori; its whakapapa and how it came to Aotearoa; the mōhiotanga (science of knowledge) of planting and harvesting; and how to cook, preserve and store kūmara. One of the most affecting aspects of this kōrero was Williams' grandmother teaching him how to store the kūmara and how to handle it—'be kind'.

Williams tells us that his grandparents taught him how to build a rua kūmara (a kūmara pit) into the side of a hill:

> The design of the pit was an engineering feat ... the design genius of tīpuna in the management and cohabitation with the environment, the algorithms and science for living with nature handed down over generations. The inside of the pit, when fully closed up, was airtight. This created a vacuum, which kept the precious tubers bone-dry.

Near the end of this story we learn of an old kūmara pit that was unearthed in 2006 with a cache of perfectly preserved kūmara that had been abandoned fifty years earlier: 'The tubers were covered in bracken fern and mānuka brush and had remained untouched by moisture, sunlight or air.' 'So … the kūmara … it was not only about planting, it was also about storytelling.'

He rua kūmara tēnei taonga. The kūmara pit seems a fitting kupu whakarite (metaphor) by which to describe the mix of genres within the book, which, like the rua kūmara, is a treasured storehouse containing carefully turned and curated narratives and poems, each a perfectly preserved and rich source of intellectual and spiritual nourishment.

The kūmara also ties into one of the themes that echoes throughout the many poems in this book: the natural environment, Rangi and Papa, Papatūānuku and her importance to Māori. Many other themes weaving through Williams' writing are based on his experiences as an activist, teacher and writer—topics such as colonisation, Te Tiriti, the Tūhoe raids, land marches and protests. As Ihimaera writes of Williams: 'He rite ki te kōpara e kōkō nei i te ata. His kōrero is like listening to the bellbird singing at dawn.'

I recommend this book to all readers interested in the wisdom, poetry and insight of a respected kaumātua with a mastery of poetry and prose.

Tree Sense: Ways of thinking about trees is an anthology of essays, artworks and poetry by artists, activists, ecologists and advocates, each of whom has 'a deep respect for trees'. This is a book for people interested in the environment, and—as editor Susette Goldsmith admits—to a certain extent it will 'preach to the converted'.

I am one of the converted, and I was both excited and a little apprehensive about reading this book. Excited because I love learning about trees; apprehensive because I have some knowledge of the devastating impact humans have had and continue to have on trees in Aotearoa. The reasoning behind the legislative framework that allows the wanton destruction of trees in suburban Auckland is set out in Mels Barton's piece, 'Our Lost Trees'. Barton suggests Aotearoa is 'definitely well behind best practice in retaining urban forest cover … the Tree Council estimates that we have lost one-third of Auckland's tree cover since the Resource Management Act 1991 (RMA) reforms were implemented in 2015 and general tree protection was removed. Until this tree protection measure is reinstated, the destruction will continue.'

At times I was soothed and at other times saddened by what this book reveals about trees in Aotearoa. In this respect *Tree Sense* succeeds in what it sets out to do in talking about humans through the medium of trees. Part One, titled 'Needful Dependency'—a phrase taken from Elizabeth Smither's poem 'Tree breath and human' that appears at the beginning of the book—focuses on 'the various characteristics of trees'. Here

Glynn Church's essay provides captivating facts about tree life in Aotearoa that many who live here may not know. For example, I was unaware that tree ferns like ponga and mamaku are relics of the dinosaur era. I also didn't know that the māhoe is the largest violet in the world! Such gems are peppered throughout the book and make me want to head into the bush to find examples of these trees and look at them anew.

Many pieces in Part One are informative and uplifting. In her essay 'A Line Between Two Trees/Observations from the Critical Zone', Ann Noble asks, 'Do trees talk?' In an attempt to answer this question, she buried a length of photographic film in the earth in 'the Critical Zone'—among the roots between two trees—in the hope of 'capturing some form of tree language'. The results appear in an astonishing eight-page fold-out image that records a kind of tracery reminiscent of wood and canopy and stars. The image effectively enhances the book's message, as do the beautiful black-and-white illustrations of trees by botanical artist Nancy M. Adams that adorn the cover and appear at the beginning of each written piece.

Part Two, 'Greening the Anthropocene', takes a 'lead from the past and provides some guidelines for the future'. The pieces here contain some of the more depressing content. Susette Goldsmith's essay 'Burying the Axe and the Fire-stick' examines the 1940 centennial of the signing of Te Tiriti o Waitangi. Centennial activities included the planting of more than '300,000 native and many thousands of exotic trees, shrubs, grasses and herbs propagated by schools', and '220,000 trees by local authorities, institutions and individuals'. While those activities are not saddening in themselves—indeed, all are about rejuvenation—the worrying thing is that so much planting needed to occur in the first place. And here we connect to the legacy of 100 years of colonial settlement in Aotearoa and the advent of the 'axe and the fire-stick' that led to problems of 'landslides, floods, erosion, silting, spread of scrub and weeds and serious shortage of timber'. The 'vexed question of natives versus exotics' is a recurrent theme throughout the collection, as is Eurocentrism when it comes to the definition of an 'acceptable tree', as discussed in Colin D. Meurk's piece, 'Think Like a Mataī'.

As the media preview says, this book is perfect for dipping into. It is a collection that honours trees, the 'largest visible organisms on the planet'; that talks about trees as storytellers, as ancient analogies for humans, as life-giving providers of oxygen.

I recommend this book to all who have any relationship with or interest in our environment and the trees around us. Whether you know it or not, you are bound to trees. As Kennedy Warne writes, 'Trees are our kin. We share a sacred bond.'

Both books capture the wisdom of our elders. Both speak of the importance of the land, the natural environment and voices we need to pay attention to in so many ways.

Six of the Best

Charlotte Grimshaw

Six by Six: Short stories by New Zealand's best writers, edited by Bill Manhire (Victoria University Press, 2021), 560pp, $40

One day recently, when we were in the middle of a discussion about the current pandemic, perhaps the Delta surge we'd just overcome in Auckland or the projected peak of the Omicron wave, my mother's expression turned glazed and distant and she began to describe another pandemic in another time: the polio outbreak in her childhood that closed the schools, setting her and her sisters and friends free to roam and run wild for a whole summer. And it was, she said, now she remembered it, an exceptionally long, hot summer like the drought in Auckland in 2020 and 2021, when the parks turned brown, the streams dried up, the skies every day were cloudless blue; and for her, back then, there was nothing to be done but swim and bike for miles and dream your way through another day, a gang of kids liberated from the world of school and clocks and teachers and parents, just for a time. The adults must have been fearful (infantile paralysis, the horrifying threat of the 'iron lung': what could be more terrifying for a parent?) but she remembered it as dreamy, idyllic, timeless, mercifully free from the tyranny of phones and computers and Zoom. No Google school, no remote learning; you could read a book under a tree, and other than that, some lessons might arrive in the mail every now and then.

Her sudden intense recall struck me on a number of fronts. It was a vivid memory of a pandemic in her lifetime (stop worrying; there's nothing new under the sun; Covid too shall pass). It sounded so lovely (every cloud, et cetera). It gave one a tiny, no doubt irrational hope about climate change (she's very old and she remembers an intense drought; maybe the disturbing lack of rain in Auckland is normal). And most particularly it struck me because I was reading *Six by Six*, the anthology of short stories by six New Zealand writers edited by Bill Manhire, and I was right in the middle of 'The Reservoir' by Janet Frame.

'The days became unbearably long and hot,' Frame wrote in 'The Reservoir'. 'Rumours circled the burning world. The sea was drying up, soon you could paddle or walk to Australia.' And later, 'The earth crackled in the early-autumn haze and still the February sun dried the world ...'

The children of Frame's story are waiting for school, but it will not start: 'Then swiftly, suddenly, disease came to the town. Infantile Paralysis. Black headlines in the paper, listing the number of cases, the number of deaths. Children everywhere, out in the country, up north, down south, two streets away.'

And so, the children of 'The Reservoir' are set free to roam. They're allowed to play along and in the creek, but the specific warning they are given each day is never to go as far as the Reservoir, which is upstream and distant and regarded as very dangerous. It comes to represent, for the children, the place of mystery they must eventually reach if they're ever to find meaning in the adult-controlled world through which they move.

'The Reservoir' is a terrific narrative, one of many in this rich and vivid collection by six wildly different New Zealand writers. Each story is idiosyncratic and fascinating and an entertainment in itself, and at the same time each adds to the interesting, inevitable impression created by the grouping of six by six: you can't help comparing, and noticing which writer might be said to outdo the next—aesthetically, stylistically, verbally.

As an impression it's slightly unfair, in that the comparison depends on the selection of stories, which, it could be argued (as a matter of subjective taste), doesn't necessarily represent some of the writers' best, most shining work. This is a newly released set of the original story collection, now a VUP Classic. The stories were chosen in order to represent the range of tones and styles of each writer, also the development of talent, rather than simply picking out the greatest hits. The result is a highly entertaining and uneven mix, with undeniable classics alongside some messy mixtures of genius, charm, humour and hilarity—and the odd crashing dud.

The stories are highly visual and if, for that reason, the imaginative impression is of a gallery (this was how the collection kept representing itself to me), the most polished and complete, the most unassailably perfect, classic and transcendent works on display are the stories of Katherine Mansfield. With time as the judge, she stands apart. You can't beat the quality of the writing, the insight, the shimmer behind the words, the wry, intelligent humour in every line and, most emphatic of all, the beauty. Aesthetically, verbally, the stories of Katherine Mansfield are beautiful—and peerless.

Mansfield comes first in the collection, followed by Frank Sargeson with his sharp wit and his acerbic asides and sly expressions of hidden violence and sexuality. His segment opens with the genius of 'Conversation with My Uncle'. It's all much more rugged and rough, not such a flattering selection perhaps, as if stronger stories could have been included than 'The Undertaker's Story' and 'Just Trespassing, Thanks'.

Maurice Duggan's section starts low key with 'A Small Story', progresses into the languidly vivid comic genius of 'Along Rideout Road That Summer' and proceeds to the creaking, camp weirdness of 'O'Leary's Orchard', in which old O'Leary, with gaunt humour, seduces the delectable Isobel Bernstein whose mother drives a Bentley, among other strange and random details. There's a constant tone, hard to define, maybe a kind of blackly laughing, drunken hilarity to Duggan's stories.

Then there's Janet Frame, and along with 'The Reservoir' we get 'Solutions', a story that starts out with a coy tone and becomes increasingly disturbing until it turns nasty and positively upsetting; it feels horribly claustrophobic and surreal, like an insight into serious mental distress. Frame's 'The Bull Calf' is a moving portrayal of a girl facing society's prudishness and cruelty, and the sharp and witty 'You Are Now Entering the Human Heart' includes a very funny description of a schoolteacher's encounter with a snake.

The best of Patricia Grace's selected six is 'Valley', a rural story covering the four seasons, full of lyrical observations of nature and children, and small, poignantly beautiful moments. There's a strong story about birth, 'Between Earth and Sky', and the charming 'Waimarie', in which an old woman goes to a tangi.

Grace has successfully embraced the vernacular, sometimes so successfully and thoroughly it becomes a challenge to the inner ear. This is from 'Kahawai':

> It's only us who don't go. Sometimes. Or don't get up. Right? Because of hangovers, or laziness or going somewhere else. Or from not being back from somewhere. Only us have sickies. Right? But anyway ... Good. Good on yous. Kahawai, yum. Make some bread too. Yahoo.

And this from Grace's 'The Wall', about a group of men building a wall:

> We all scrapped over which rock. That one. Nah. Ha, ha, haw, haw, like that. They try them out to see which one. A lot of times my rock was the good one, fitted in just right, ha, ha, ha, hee, hee, get stuffed. Hee, hee, ha, ha. Haw, haw, haw. It was only easy after a while.

The story goes on and on in that vein. It raises the memory of Martin Amis's iconoclastic comment about a passage in one of Joan Didion's classic works: 'I find this style of writing as resonant as a pop-gun.'

Owen Marshall has some excellent stories in the collection, especially 'A Day With Yesterman', in which he gives us the thoroughly likeable character of Chatterton, a man making the best of a very good day. It's a story with Marshall's characteristic laconic charm and good-natured humour, even a kind of sweetness. 'A Poet's Dream of Amazons', the tragic story of a poet who lies dying in his parents' laundry, is really funny, with none of the darkness and violence running through some of Marshall's work.

Reviewers sometimes advise cosily of books like *Six by Six*: 'Enjoy dipping in and out. Read a story here and there. Any order will do.' I would say this: Do not dip in and out. Read each writer's six stories strictly in order. Do not stop until you've finished. Enjoy each writer's work for its idiosyncratic strangeness, its strengths and weaknesses. When you've finished the whole book, compare the six, openly, generously, ruthlessly. Enjoy the judgements you come to. Find a whole extra layer of interest in the comparisons you're able to make.

A Rich, Layered Sense of Context

Helen Watson White

Helen Kelly: Her life by Rebecca Macfie (Awa Press, 2021), 410pp, $49.99

'We don't need low wages in this country,' said Helen Kelly on becoming president of the Council of Trade Unions (CTU) in 2007. 'There's no excuse for it. People should be able to go to work, work their hours and have a decent standard of living at the end of the week.'

It sounds so simple, and to the Kellys it was. Rebecca Macfie's action-packed and deeply thoughtful biography, *Helen Kelly: Her life*, is less one person's story and more the biography of a radical family. Macfie shows us how, in the Wellington setting of parliamentarians, publicans and pundits, Kelly and her parents, Cath and Pat, always knew what they wanted but also what they were up against. Knowing where the trade union movement came from made their joint trajectory sure, throughout the second half of the twentieth century. In the new millennium, Kelly continued the work for another sixteen years until her death from cancer when she was in her prime.

Macfie gives a fascinating chapter to each of Kelly's parents, showing how their different backgrounds contributed to Kelly's make-up, her way of operating and the strength of her beliefs. Pat, 'of Irish Catholic descent with little formal education', was an English immigrant from the Liverpool docklands, born in 1929 above the office of the Scalers' Union. His dockworker father struggled through the Depression with no regular employment, the family surviving on 'parish relief, weekly loans from the local pawn shop, and the mutual support of neighbours'. Life was what you made of it, together—*together* being the operative word.

At the other end of the social scale, the author describes Cath's paternal grandfather, Max Eichelbaum, son of a 'wealthy East Prussian Jewish merchant', who moved his large family to Wellington and set up house in Thorndon. Cath's parents, Siegfried and Vera, married in 1915 and were 'well known in Wellington's professional and academic circles'; Cath, born in 1926, became a university student with a goal to 'improve the world'. She had travelled abroad and seen much of life—and of left-wing activism—before marrying Pat in 1960.

Life and work were one and the same for this pair. The day before Cath gave birth to Helen in 1964, she was selling the Communist paper the *People's Voice* and distributing anti-war pamphlets to factory workers in Kaiwharawhara. Pat, who was city organiser for the Wellington Drivers Union, would push Kelly and her older brother Max in a 'cart made of apple boxes and old pram wheels' to visit fellow unionists on the waterfront.

Macfie describes the warmth and solidarity of the Kelly establishment—Cath's house in Shannon Street, Mount Victoria—where friends and allies in the Labour movement were welcomed like family. Snapshots reveal how the neighbours' kids became extra siblings for Helen and Max and joined the Kelly cousins on holidays. At home there was ongoing discussion about international affairs or current issues affecting workers' families. The future leader of the CTU was thus educated from an early age by being immersed in her parents' political lives. In one of Macfie's hundreds of recorded interviews, Kelly describes her father as 'passionate about safety for drivers'. Always wanting to be at the nub of an issue, 'He would go out in the middle of the night and photograph crashed trucks.'

Kelly's closeness to her parents meant that youthful rebellion would have been beside the point, writes Macfie. They were a team. The focus was always on the larger fight on behalf of workers, not just for higher wages but for recognition as equal citizens and improvement in their working conditions, under employment laws that never stayed the same. For the twenty years from 1984 to Pat's death in 2004, Kelly's ability to effect change, and her awareness of the need for it, meant she was on the same page as her parents, if working in different fields.

Single-minded as the Kellys were, a book encompassing the lives of four generations becomes, with Macfie's addition of a rich, layered sense of context, almost a history of the period. Her building of the larger picture begins with the rise of Fascism and its effect on the Eichelbaums. Identifying the Cold War origins of New Zealand's crusade of union-bashing, 1951–1991 and after, Macfie analyses the era of protest that unfolded alongside it, introducing the personalities involved in what seemed for the Left an unending battle with a many-headed foe.

Sometimes the battle became physical. In 1984 a terrorist bomb was exploded in Wellington's Trades Hall, causing the death of caretaker Ernie Abbott, a Kelly family friend and lifelong servant of the Labour movement. Pat, then head of the Cleaners' Union, was meeting with others at Trades Hall to discuss Muldoon's wage freeze. When Kelly, then aged nineteen and a second-year student at Teachers' College, first heard the news, she was horrified that the person killed could have been her father. Left-leaning leaders were often the target of abuse and threats, writes Macfie, as anti-union forces intensified over the decade following National's notorious 1975 election advertisements. As Pat thundered at Abbott's funeral, someone driven by this 'hatred' had committed the ultimate outrage, 'striking down a man who was going about his ordinary work'. This shocking event focused the Kellys on a drive to change the government.

After teaching for two years, in 1989 Kelly took up the work the author feels she was 'born to': a half-time job with each of two early childhood education (ECE) unions, which began at odds but later merged. In Rosslyn Noonan and Sonja Davies she had excellent role models; her colleagues recognised her strong 'sense of mission' and impatience to improve life for workers who were often unqualified and invariably underpaid.

As Macfie tells the story, history and power seemed to abandon people like those ECE workers in the course of the 1980s and 1990s, as Labour's Roger Douglas ushered in what she calls the neoliberal economics 'revolution'. Then in 1991, the year in which Ruth Richardson cut social welfare benefits, the incoming National government dealt what was intended as a final blow to the union movement. The proposed Employment Contracts Bill individualised the contract between employer and employee and took away collective bargaining and worker supports. Macfie describes the 'divisions and bitterness' among the unions as they tried to prevent it coming into law: 'The merger of the Federation of Labour and Combined State Unions to form the CTU had been supposed to achieve a single, unified voice for working people, but it was far from it.' Setting the issue in a wider context, she quotes the radio programme *Insight* warning that New Zealand's unions 'would have fewer rights than in any other country in the developed world'.

While this crisis for organised labour comes less than halfway through the book, by this point in the reading we have already seen a determination and resourcefulness in Kelly that will carry her unscathed through many further battles. In 1994 she was hired as an organiser for the Association of University Staff (AUS), in a climate Macfie describes as profoundly changed by free-market economics, government cuts and a policy of 'user-pays'. Kelly was not deterred. She was at home in the education sector, and in 1999, having returned to work for the NZEI (the primary teachers' union), she helped achieve pay parity for primary and secondary teachers, something Rosslyn Noonan called 'one of the great negotiating victories in New Zealand trade union history'. Macfie describes it as 'a rare success in a landscape of defeat'.

There are a number of stories going on at the same time in this book, which gives it a rough, recognisable humanity. There's work and there's unpaid work; Kelly was always multi-tasking. Having 'footslogged' for Labour in 1996 while studying part-time for a law degree, she ran Marian Hobbs' campaign for Wellington Central in 1999. By 2002, as general secretary of the AUS, she had joined the CTU's governing council, and in 2003 Pat and Cath saw her elected vice-president of the CTU. Pat died shortly after of heart disease caused by 'decades of roll-your-owns and beer'. His funeral in 2004, like Ernie Abbott's, was a big event in Wellington; co-unionist Dave Morgan eulogised a man who was 'funny, generous, wise, selfless, dedicated, determined, argumentative, loving, revolutionary and inspirational'.

Kelly was now leading the 6000-member AUS, a role in which she was not universally trusted. The author has interviewed a range of participants, some of whom found Kelly 'ambitious and driven' or 'stroppy', others 'gregarious and vivacious'. It was a difficult job, as Macfie observes: 'Salary bargaining was a zero-sum game: if staff got pay rises, something else would have to be cut.' University staff were not natural unionists and had to be persuaded to pull together. After a year of nervous talks and another Labour-won election in 2005, a 'significant bargaining development' led to an extra $61 million being released to fund increases in university pay. Again Macfie finds that, in choosing CTU's president in 2007, some unionists supported Kelly while others did not; what won out was her ability to unite people and to 'think outside the square'.

The author's ironic chapter headings mark a trail of cost-cutting issues following the Global Financial Crisis. 'Lucky to Have a Job', which opens with the story of a young security guard killed on his first nightshift, refers to the common notion that employers are doing people a favour by giving them work and have no further responsibility. 'Dangerous By Design' exposes major breaches of workplace safety with employers in denial—the most notorious being the death of twenty-nine men at Pike River Mine. Kelly's narrative throughout the aftermath was that, at the very least, these workers should have been protected from danger—let alone death. They were not. Her support of the bereaved was timely and heartfelt, observes Macfie.

The solidarity process—Kelly's Jacinda-like embracing of an issue and of the people it affected—was repeated as the numbers of men killed in forestry mounted every year. Her actions (and this book) were based on thorough research, data-gathering and meetings with people on the ground. Poignant photographs memorialise the men who went to work in dangerous places where safety was not included in the expectations of the employer or the job's design. Macfie relates how Kelly became the face of this national disaster: anguished, critical, passionate about the need for change—and, through her position, able to effect it.

Colleagues in the education unions had called her 'unstoppable'. The chapter title 'Fight to the Last' refers to the many campaigns—run concurrently—that merged Kelly's 'life' and 'work' in a seven-day marathon, every week for decades. But it also refers to the cancer that changed everything.

If you thought this book would be hagiography, or merely a catalogue of disputes, think again. Written by a senior award-winning journalist, it is packed with potent images, drama, storytelling, humour and realism. Quite simply, it is one of the best books I have read.

REVIEW ESSAY

The Frankness of Strangers

Kerry Lane

A discussion of place, space and **Out Here: An anthology of Takatāpui and LGBTQIA+ writers from Aotearoa,** edited by Chris Tse and Emma Barnes (Auckland University Press, 2021), 368pp, $49.99

> It was when the beach boy told him quickly, confessionally, with the complete frankness of strangers who meet accidentally and know they are unlikely to see each other again, his life story.
> —Peter Wells, from 'Sweet Nothing'

Out Here is an imposing book, a large, heavy hardback with a bright cover, white and rainbow. You couldn't slip it into a pocket or read it discreetly on the bus. It's bold. It's out and proud.

The subtitle describes the book as an anthology of takatāpui and LGBTQIA+ writers from Aotearoa. The introduction by editors Chris Tse and Emma Barnes explains further:

> We'd originally set out to provide a view of queer writing in New Zealand published from 1985 onwards, but the end result is something that is much more representative of the growth and increased visibility of queer writers being published over the last ten to fifteen years.

The first impression when flipping through is somewhat cacophonous. It certainly delivers on its initial concept as 'a riot of brightness, life and feelings'. Kalee Jackson's design work is beautiful from cover to cover, and the book is immaculate in its presentation of sensible prose, wild experiments with poetic form, comics, playscript, and just about every other way words can be arranged on a page.

Specifically, the editors wanted pieces to 'not only focus on queer life events like coming out or first love' but also 'smaller things, bigger things, different things, to see narratives that aren't always shown for people like us'. Nevertheless, the pieces must, by definition, be 'queer writing'. Work by queer writers, then? Well, maybe—the first couple of pages of the introduction are largely devoted to discussion of the way that various critically and commercially successful writers from the New Zealand literary canon have not been considered as queer writers or through a queer lens. I'm not sure it's fair to define a writer through the lenses by which others read their work. Is a queer writer more queer if others treat them as such?

The editors go on to clarify: 'It's not our intention to present a canon or a tidy history or to make a definitive statement of what contemporary queer New Zealand writing is right now. We wanted to collect as many of us together as we could, but we know there are some absences ...' The task Tse and Barnes have taken up is a monumental one, and I applaud what they have achieved. *Out Here* is a beautiful book, and it has introduced me to many writers whose work I had not previously encountered. From their description of the selection process, it seems the editors had a clear intuitive sense of what they were looking for, even if it was difficult to summarise neatly.

The overarching question of what this book is makes it difficult to discuss. Given the introduction's focus on the lenses with which the wider culture examines queer writing, perhaps it's worth looking at how *Out Here* has been received and described by others. Carole Beu, cited in the book's media release, says, 'It's the past and future. It's a taonga. These writers have claimed their space. Let's celebrate their voices!' Jean Sergent, writing for *The Spinoff*, describes 'holding the space for queerness in art, theatre and literature in Aotearoa [as] an ecstatic privilege'. The book's media release refers to 'space ... to tell stories'.

Again and again, we come back to this idea: the book is a space. The book is a space. The book is a space.

What does it mean for a community if its spaces are not physical spaces? The rise of the internet and social media has made it easier for queer people to find each other, but this has also made it easier for us to exist in social worlds that are entirely dislocated from physical space. A similar shift to digital community has happened rapidly for many other groups in the last two years—and few people would claim it is an equivalent way of finding that sense of belonging that drives us all. After having our communities shifted beneath us, it's fair to say we are in the middle of a reckoning with the very idea of space.

I believe a shift towards digital space also creates a shift in the way we understand communities as existing in time. Dislocated from the physical world, some things become more transient, some more permanent. The pieces in this collection are not dated; they have been set adrift from the physical, political, social and economic context in which they were written. The effect is diverse and, in some places, exhilarating, but it also limits the extent to which the pieces can be understood in conversation with one another.

The writing collected in *Out Here* is arranged in alphabetical order by authors' first names rather than by theme, identity or chronology. The effect is jarring at first; this jigsawing of form and subject seems to highlight difference rather than commonality. Reading on, however, we sense how subtle eddies of shared experience begin to appear. Just like the commentators, the writers keep coming back to space:

a longing for physical, not metaphorical, place is the closest thing the collection has to a unifying theme. Not any one place specifically, or even Aotearoa more generally: there are works here from the USA, the Pacific Islands, Sri Lanka. These places are specific, concrete and deeply personal in the details chosen to bring them to life. Gina Cole's 'Melt' stands out to me for the elegant precision in its depiction of Howick, where my grandparents lived when I was growing up. This particular piece also highlights the fact that a preoccupation with place is inextricable today from a preoccupation with climate and, in Aotearoa, with colonisation. All of these threads come back to questions of the physicality of belonging, what it means to be and belong as a body in a space—as *these* bodies in *this* space.

Unlike Aotearoa, the USA, the Pacific Islands or Sri Lanka, a book is not defined by the activities of the people who live, work, hail from or congregate in an area. A book, if it is a space, is shaped by curatorial decisions, including definition of its links to both time and the physical world. I will not pretend that the curation of the spaces in which we interact is entirely new; there are plenty of places where only certain people are allowed to go. A licensed bar is a curated space in this sense, as is the world outside a prison. In another sense, we curate ourselves in different ways in different spaces. Whether we are submitting our writing to an anthology or making small talk with a co-worker, we make choices about the version of ourselves that we wish to be in the given context.

In the situation of a conversation with a colleague, these choices are made moment-by-moment in response to those around you, and are generally not limited to a significant extent by the curation of a third party. In an anthology—or a Facebook group—this is not quite the case. These are what I will call 'remote spaces': nonphysical and not anchored to physical location, atemporal to varying degrees, and implicitly or explicitly curated by third parties. The distinction between remote and non-remote space exists on a spectrum; a collection like *Out Here* is absolutely less remote than a crowded global chat server.

That said, Covid-19 has accelerated a cultural shift along this spectrum towards ever-greater remoteness in the spaces where we spend most of our time. We see this at work, where we may only ever communicate with colleagues through administrated software suites; in the arts and exercise classes that have been replaced by pre-recorded YouTube videos; and in our social communities which, like the queer community, may increasingly be defined by their expressions in remote space.

This brings us back to the question of purpose. Remote spaces have a reason for their existence, and the creation of healthy, stable community is often secondary or entirely absent. The purpose of many digital spaces is to generate advertising revenue or to mine commercially valuable data. What does it do to a community, to be pruned and shaped according to such a purpose?

Out Here, along with other similar anthologies, is both less remote and less commercial in purpose than many digital spaces, but it is still highly curated and distinctly atemporal. People, relationships and community exist in time but a single printed anthology must, by its nature, capture a snapshot moment, or else flatten many into one. As a literary collection it also has an aesthetic purpose, and in their introduction the editors acknowledge that their own tastes and stylistic preferences have necessarily shaped the contents. It is not a book with the sole goal of complete and accurate documentary.

Decisions about where to step forward and back when curating a project like this are tricky. In this case, the social context of the collection invites socio-political as well as aesthetic analysis, whether or not this is invited or justified. Hera Lindsay Bird in 'Untitled 404' says, 'I don't think the great project of art is ideological messaging,' and this must surely be even truer when the raw material for a project is the words of others.

For my part, I wish the editors would remain present as I move through the introduction to the book's contents. I want to know which pieces were sought out and which came from the call for submissions. Who chose and trimmed the excerpts from longer works, or chose the pieces from those writers who are no longer with us—Heather McPherson and Peter Wells? Why *these* works and not others?

Above all, I am curious about pieces that *aren't* here. What did the editors say no to, and why? And I want to ask the writers how *they* chose what to submit. Are the pieces they selected more representative, more queer? Who never saw the call for submissions; and who saw it and felt it wasn't for them, and why? Some types of writing are conspicuous in their absence: Jessica Niurangi Mary Maclean's 'Kāore e wehi tōku kiri ki te taraongaonga; my skin does not fear the nettle' is the only one in the anthology that takes the form of an academic essay. Was it the only work of this kind that was submitted, or were others received and discarded?

In essence, the book makes me crave conversation in a way that is made impossible by its nature as a remote space. This separation from interaction, this sense of listening and looking without being able to respond, is also apparent in the work of some of the younger writers. Young adulthood is a time characterised by introspection, yes, but there is also a thread of profound, existential loneliness here, as in Cadence Chung's 'The End': 'I'll be … busy staring at my crush's icon when / they broadcast the Great Flood (and subsequent rapture) over a Zoom meeting.' How many of these young writers know any of the older writers in the collection in person, or know queer people from different generations at all?

The media release references these young writers specifically:

> … the cacophony of voices brought together in *Out Here* sing out loud and proud, ensuring that future generations of queers are afforded the space to tell their stories and be themselves without fear of retribution or harm.

We have more opportunity than ever to speak out into the vastness of the internet, but where do we go now to actually talk to one another? This section of the media release is quoted almost directly from the book's introduction, but not quite; the same passage, near the end of the introduction, attributes this creation of space not to the book itself or to the cacophony of voices but to 'those who continue to step forward and put in the mahi'. *Out Here* is tangible evidence that Tse and Barnes, like many of the anthology's contributors, have made the choice to pour their time and energy into this community and the people in it, yet they stand apart from many commentators in choosing not to describe the book as a space.

A book is not a physical space—but its editorial room is, and so are the kitchens and gardens and rivers and workplaces that are tenderly sketched in its pages. A book may not be a space at all, but it can be a window into one, and *Out Here* is a window to many.

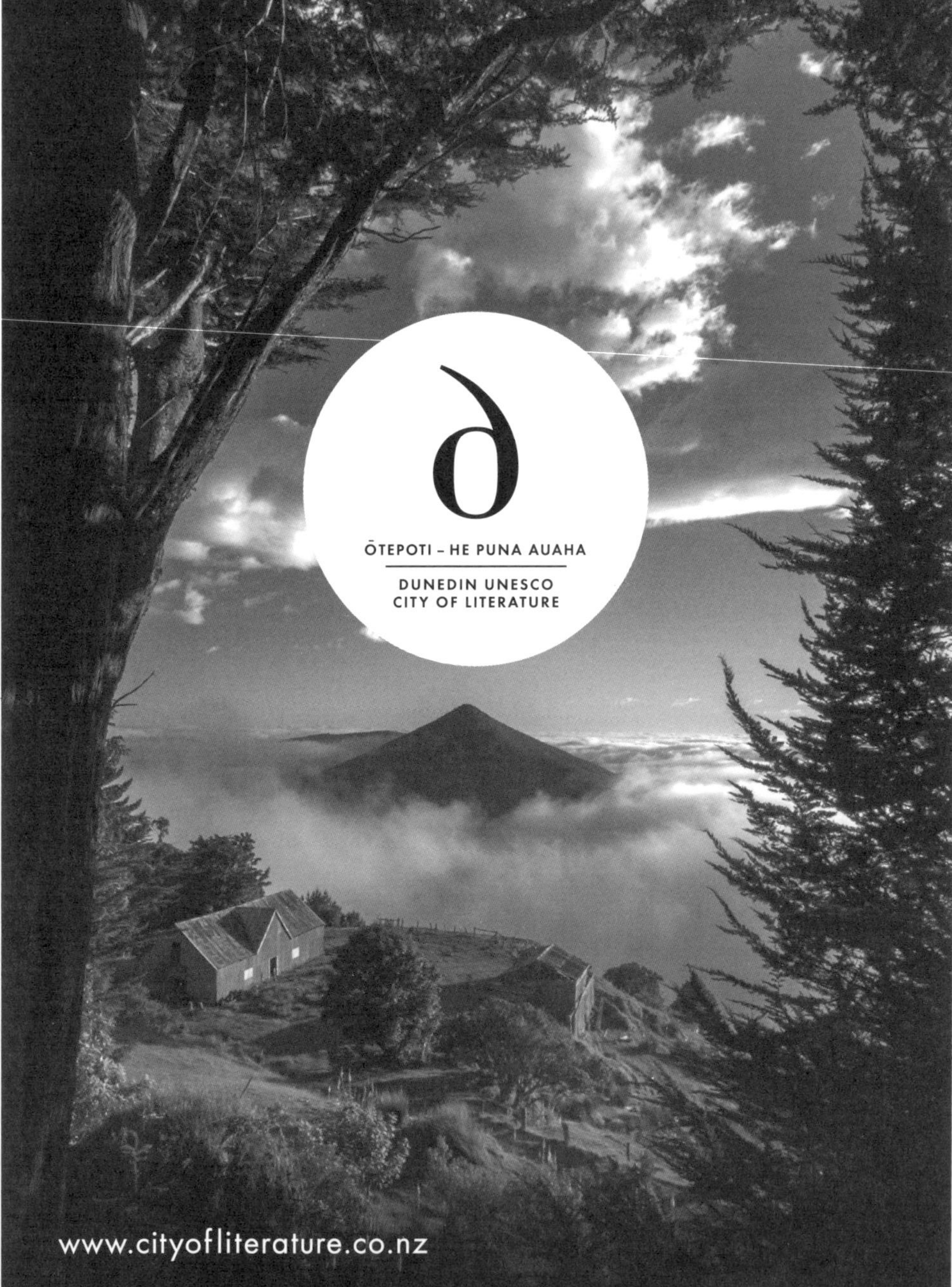
ŌTEPOTI – HE PUNA AUAHA
DUNEDIN UNESCO
CITY OF LITERATURE
www.cityofliterature.co.nz

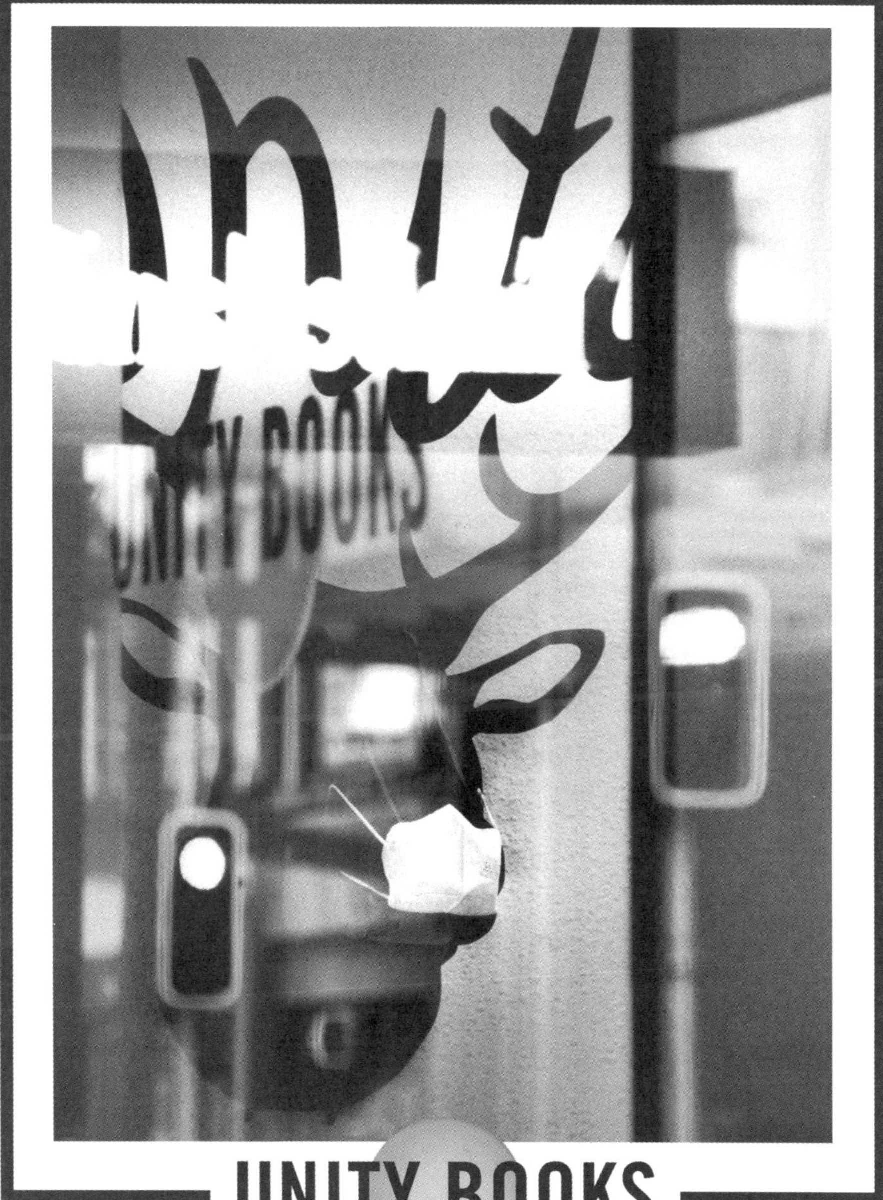

CONTRIBUTORS

Philip Armstrong's poetry collection *Sinking Lessons* (Otago University Press, 2020) won the 2019 Kathleen Grattan Poetry Award. His work has appeared in *Landfall*, *Snorkel*, *PN Review*, *takahē* and elsewhere.

Caroline Barron (Ngāti Whātua, Te Uri o Hau) is an award-winning memoir and fiction writer, manuscript assessor, book reviewer and creative writing teacher. Her debut, *Ripiro Beach: A memoir of life after near death*, won the 2020 New Zealand Heritage Literary Award for Best Non-fiction Book. She has an MA in creative writing from the University of Auckland.

Cindy Botha lives in Tauranga and began reading and writing poetry at a late age while caring for her mother, who suffers from dementia. Her work has since been published in New Zealand, the UK and the US.

Chris Cantillon lives in Whanganui and works in Marton.

Brent Cantwell is from Timaru and lives with his family in the hinterland of Queensland. He teaches high-school English and has been writing for pleasure for 24 years. He has recently been published in *Sweet Mammalian*, *Milly Magazine*, *Poetry New Zealand*, *Landfall*, *foam:e* and *takahē*.

Marisa Cappetta has published widely in journals and anthologies. *How to Tour the World on a Flying Fox* was published by Steele Roberts Aotearoa (2016). *Windows Below the Waterline* is due in 2022.

Lucy Chen is a junior doctor training in obstetrics and gynaecology. She grew up in West Auckland and enjoys gardening, pottery and classical music. Her favourite board game is Scrabble.

Alastair Clarke is a New Zealand writer who is re-seeing the country after a long absence. Most recently his work has been published in *Antipodes*, the *Poetry New Zealand Yearbook* and *Fresh Ink*.

Gina Cole is a freelance writer of Fijian, Scottish and Welsh descent. Her collection *Black Ice Matter* (Huia Publishers, 2016) won Best First Book of Fiction at the 2017 Ockham New Zealand Book Awards. Her forthcoming science fiction fantasy novel *Na Viro* (Huia Publishers, 2022) is a work of Pasifikafuturism.

Jennifer Compton is a New Zealander living in Australia. Recent Work Press in Canberra published her eleventh book of poetry, *the moment, taken*, in 2021.

Molly Crighton is an English student at the University of Otago. Her work can be found in *Starling*, *Landfall*, *takahē*, *a fine line*, *The Cormorant* and *Re-Draft*.

Helena de Bres writes creative nonfiction and teaches philosophy. *Artful Truths: The philosophy of memoir* was published by the University of Chicago Press in 2021, and she's currently writing a personal essay collection about twins.

Bill (William) Direen's poems can be found online and in journals. A book-length poem, *New Sea Land*, appeared in 2005. A songwriter and performer, Bill has completed a tetralogy of experimental writings with poetic content, entitled *Enclosures*. For 11 years he edited the cross-cultural literary journal *Percutio*. In 2021 he edited an anthology of work by writers opposed to mass book disposals at the National Library of New Zealand. He lives in Dunedin.

Murray Edmond's *Time to Make a Song and Dance: Cultural revolt in Auckland in the 1960s* (Atuanui Press) was published in 2021. Forthcoming in 2022 are *FARCE* and *Sandbank Sonnets: A memoir*, both from Compound Press.

David Eggleton is a poet, writer and critic who lives in Ōtepoti Dunedin. He is the New Zealand Poet Laureate for 2019–22.

Barbara Else (MNZM) writes for adults and children. She has been a writing fellow at Victoria and Otago universities and in 2016 was awarded the Storylines Margaret Mahy Medal in recognition of her services to children's literature.

James R Ford is a conceptual artist whose work contemplates the nature of value, the perils of choice, and the search for meaning. Ford (b. 1980) studied at Nottingham Trent University and then Goldsmiths College in England. He moved to Aotearoa New Zealand in 2009 and currently lives and works in Wellington.

Janis Freegard is the author of several poetry collections, most recently *Reading the Signs* (The Cuba Press, 2020) and a novel, *The Year of Falling* (Mākaro Press, 2015). She lives in Wellington.

Charlotte Grimshaw is the author of seven novels and two short-story collections and has been shortlisted for or won many accolades, including the Montana Medal for Book of the Year. She is an award-winning reviewer and columnist, and her bestselling novels *The Night Book* and *Soon* have been made into the TV mini-series *The Bad Seed*. Her memoir, *The Mirror Book*, was published in 2021 by Penguin.

Michael Harlow has written 13 books of poetry. In 2014 he received the Lauris Edmond Memorial Award for Distinguished Contribution to Poetry in New Zealand, and in 2018 he received the Prime Minister's Award for Literary Achievement in poetry. His collections *Nothing For It But to Sing* (2016) and *The Moon in a Bowl of Water* (2019) were published by Otago University Press, and his most recent book of poems, *Renoir's Bicycle*, will be published by Cold Hub Press. Michael lives in Central Otago where he works as a Jungian psychotherapist.

Rebecca Hawkes grew up on a farm near Methven and lives in Wellington. Her poetry chapbook 'Softcore Coldsores' can be found in *AUP New Poets 5*, and her debut solo collection *Meat Lovers* will be unleashed by Auckland University Press in 2022. Rebecca is a founding member of performance popstar-poets' posse Show Ponies, and edits for the poetry journal *Sweet Mammalian*. She is co-editor of *No Other Place to Stand: An anthology of climate change poetry from Aotearoa New Zealand*, also forthcoming from AUP.

Jenna Heller writes poetry and fiction near the sea in Ōtautahi Christchurch. She is originally from the US and has called Aotearoa New Zealand home for nearly half her life.

Nathaniel Herz-Erdinger is a community organiser, chess enthusiast and sometime gardener with a passion for Chekhov, coffee, hitchhiking and Adichie. He can usually be found on Level 2 of Tūranga Library, Ōtautahi.

Zoë Higgins is a Pākehā poet of Swiss and British descent. She grew up in Horomaka and now lives and works in Pōneke. Her poetry has recently been published in *Out Here: An anthology of takatāpui and LGBTQIA+ writers from Aotearoa* (Auckland University Press, 2021).

Erik Kennedy is the author of *Another Beautiful Day Indoors* (2022) and *There's No Place Like the Internet in Springtime* (2018), both with Te Herenga Waka University Press.

Brent Kininmont lives in Tokyo. His poems can be found online, in previous issues of *Landfall* and in his collection *Thuds Underneath* (Victoria University Press, 2015).

Kerry Lane is a poet and playwright from Ōtepoti, now based in Glasgow.

Ruby Macomber is a 20-year-old Pasifika student currently studying a BA/LLB at University of Auckland. She facilitates Te Kāhui, an indigenous creative writing programme, and is fiercely passionate about equitable creative opportunities.

Maitreyabandhu has written three books on Buddhism, two poetry pamphlets and three full-length collections with Bloodaxe Books: *The Crumb Road* (2013), *Yarn* (2015) and *After Cézanne*, an illustrated meditation on the life and work of the painter (2019). He was ordained into the Triratna Buddhist Order in 1990.

Andrea Malcolm (Ātihaunui-a-Pāpārangi) lives in northwest Auckland. She has published poetry in *The Spinoff*, *takahē*, *Tarot*, the anthology *26 Letters* and as part of the Bloomsbury Festival, London.

Abigail Marshall has been featured in *Mayhem Literary Journal* and *Flash Frontier*. She is in her final year studying for a Bachelor of Arts at the University of Waikato.

Jackson Rātapu McCarthy is a poet and student from Tāmaki Makaurau. He was a finalist for the Schools Poetry Award 2021.

Sione Monū is an artist of the Tongan diaspora who lives between Canberra, Australia and Auckland. Their artwork spans the mediums of photography, moving-image, fashion and adornment, performance and drawing—exploring identity, family and pasifika queer experience in the diaspora.

Margaret Moores is an Auckland bookseller who often writes ekphrasis of photographs. Her poems and flash fiction have been published in journals and anthologies in New Zealand and Australia.

Sally J. Morgan is a Wellington-based author, artist and academic. Her debut novel, *Toto Among the Murderers* (Hachette, 2020), was longlisted for the Jann Medlicott Acorn Prize for Fiction 2021.

Emma Neale has published six novels and six poetry collections. Her first collection of short fiction, *The Pink Jumpsuit*, appeared with Quentin Wilson Publishing (2021). In 2020 she received the Lauris Edmond Memorial Award for a Distinguished Contribution to New Zealand Poetry.

Keith Nunes has had poetry, fiction, haiku and visuals published around the globe. He creates ethereal manifestations because he's inept at anything practical or useful.

Petra Nyman is a Finnish-born writer who lives in Ōtautahi Christchurch. She completed her MA in creative writing at the International Institute of Modern Letters at Victoria University of Wellington in 2020.

Jilly O'Brien has had poems published in *Landfall*, *Poetry New Zealand*, *Cordite*, *Stand*, *takahē*, *Catalyst*, *The Blue Nib*, *The Spinoff* and *Blackmail Press*, as well as anthologies worldwide. Her poetry has been displayed on the ice in Antarctica, on benches in Dunedin and on the back of parking tickets. In 2021 she was highly commended in the Caselberg Trust International Poetry competition.

Vincent O'Sullivan writes across several genres. His last poetry collection, *Things OK with You?*, came out in 2021 (Victoria University Press), and *The Dark is Light Enough*, a biography of Ralph Hotere, was published in 2020 by Penguin Random House. His new novella and short stories, *Mary's Boy, Jean-Jacques*, is just out from Te Herenga Waka University Press (2022), and his play *Small Acts of Malice* was performed in 2021. Vincent lives in Dunedin.

Claire Orchard's work has appeared in various journals and anthologies. Her first poetry collection, *Cold Water Cure*, was published by Victoria University Press in 2016.

James Pasley is from Auckland. He has an MA from the IIML, and his fiction and writing have appeared in *Landfall*, *takahē*, *Turbine*, *The Spinoff*, *Vice*, the *Sunday Star-Times* and *Business Insider*.

Kim Pieters lives and works in Dunedin. She is predominantly a nonrepresentational painter but also produces photographs, experimental film, writing and music. Her work is represented in private and public collections, including the Chartwell Collection, Auckland Art

Gallery Toi o Tāmaki, Christchurch Art Gallery Te Puna o Waiwhetū, Victoria University Collection and Dunedin Public Art Gallery.

Angela Pope is a Dunedin writer. She won the Sargeson Prize in 2020 for her short story 'Lies', and her short stories have been broadcast on RNZ.

John Prins was born in Ahuriri. He completed a Master of Creative Writing at Auckland University in 2019/20. John taught English at secondary school for six years and has recently returned to Te Matau-a-Māui to live with his family.

Kathryn Reeves is a poet and author based in Christchurch. She works as a clear communications specialist and has completed creative writing courses through the Hagley Writers' Institute and Massey University.

Brett Reid lives in Auckland Tāmaki Makaurau, where he enjoys sea swimming, cycling and reading out loud to his greyhound.

Pip Robertson lives in Wellington. She has had stories published in journals and anthologies including *Landfall*, *Reading Room*, *trampset* and *Jellyfish Review*.

Tim Saunders has had poetry and short stories published in *Turbine|Kapohau*, *takahē*, *Landfall*, *Poetry NZ Yearbook*, *Headland* and *Flash Frontier*, and won the 2018 Mindfood Magazine Short Story Competition. He placed third in the 2019 and 2020 National Flash Fiction Day Awards and was shortlisted for the 2021 Commonwealth Short Story Prize. His first book, *This Farming Life*, was published by Allen & Unwin in 2020.

Sarah Scott's poetry has appeared in *Landfall*, *Turbine|Kapohau* and *Fresh Ink*. She currently curates a Poetry Lightbox Series in Te Whanganui-a-Tara, where she lives with her partner and two sons.

Bev Stevens is a marketing and web writer/editor by day, and an emerging writer of creative nonfiction by night. Her essay 'Not Drowning But Waving' was published in *Headland* in 2021. Bev lives in Petone, has two daughters, and enjoys bush walks, reading, piano and travel.

Maggie Sturgess lives and works in Te Whanganui-a-Tara. She writes essays mostly and poetry sometimes.

Tim Upperton's second collection of poems, *The Night We Ate the Baby*, was an Ockham New Zealand Book Awards finalist in 2016. His third collection is forthcoming from Auckland University Press.

Latika Vasil lives in Wellington and is a freelance researcher and writer. Her stories have been published in anthologies and journals, including *Landfall* and *takahē*, and broadcast on RNZ. Her collection of short stories, *Rising to the Surface*, was published in 2013 by Steele Roberts Aotearoa.

Louise Wallace is the author of three collections of poetry published by Te Herenga Waka University Press, and lives in Ōtepoti Dunedin. She is the founder and editor of *Starling*, an online journal for young New Zealand writers.

Helen Watson White is a Dunedin writer with a background in university teaching, library work and editing. She has published a long list of reviews of theatre, books, music, art and opera, along with articles, short stories, poems and photographs.

Grace Yee is a poet, writer and researcher based in Melbourne. Her work has appeared in *The Spinoff*, *Hainamana*, *Overland*, *Island*, *Meanjin*, *Southerly*, *Westerly*, *Rabbit*, *Cordite Poetry Review*, the *Shanghai Literary Review*, the Women's Museum of California, *Poetry New Zealand Yearbook* and *Best of Australian Poems 2021*, among others. In 2020 Grace was awarded the Patricia Hackett Prize and the Peter Steele Poetry Award. From 2019 to 2021 she was a Creative Fellow at the State Library Victoria. Her PhD research focused on settler Chinese women's storytelling in Aotearoa New Zealand.

CONTRIBUTIONS

Landfall publishes original poems, essays, short stories, excerpts from works of fiction and non-fiction in progress, reviews, articles on the arts, and portfolios by artists. Submissions must be emailed to landfall@otago.ac.nz with 'Landfall submission' in the subject line.

Visit our website www.otago.ac.nz/press/landfall/index.html for further information.

SUBSCRIPTIONS

Landfall is published in May and November. The subscription rates for 2022 (two issues) are: New Zealand $55 (including GST); Australia $NZ65; rest of the world $NZ70. Sustaining subscriptions help to support New Zealand's longest running journal of arts and letters, and the writers and artists it showcases. These are in two categories: Friend: between $NZ75 and $NZ125 per year. Patron: $NZ250 and above.

Send subscriptions to Otago University Press, PO Box 56, Dunedin, New Zealand. For enquiries, email landfall@otago.ac.nz or call 64 3 479 8807.

Print ISBN: 978-1-99-004837-1
ePDF ISBN: 978-1-99-004839-5
ISSN 00–23–7930

Published by Otago University Press
533 Castle Street, Dunedin
New Zealand

Typeset by Otago University Press.
Printed in New Zealand by Caxton.

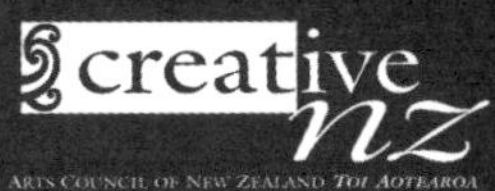

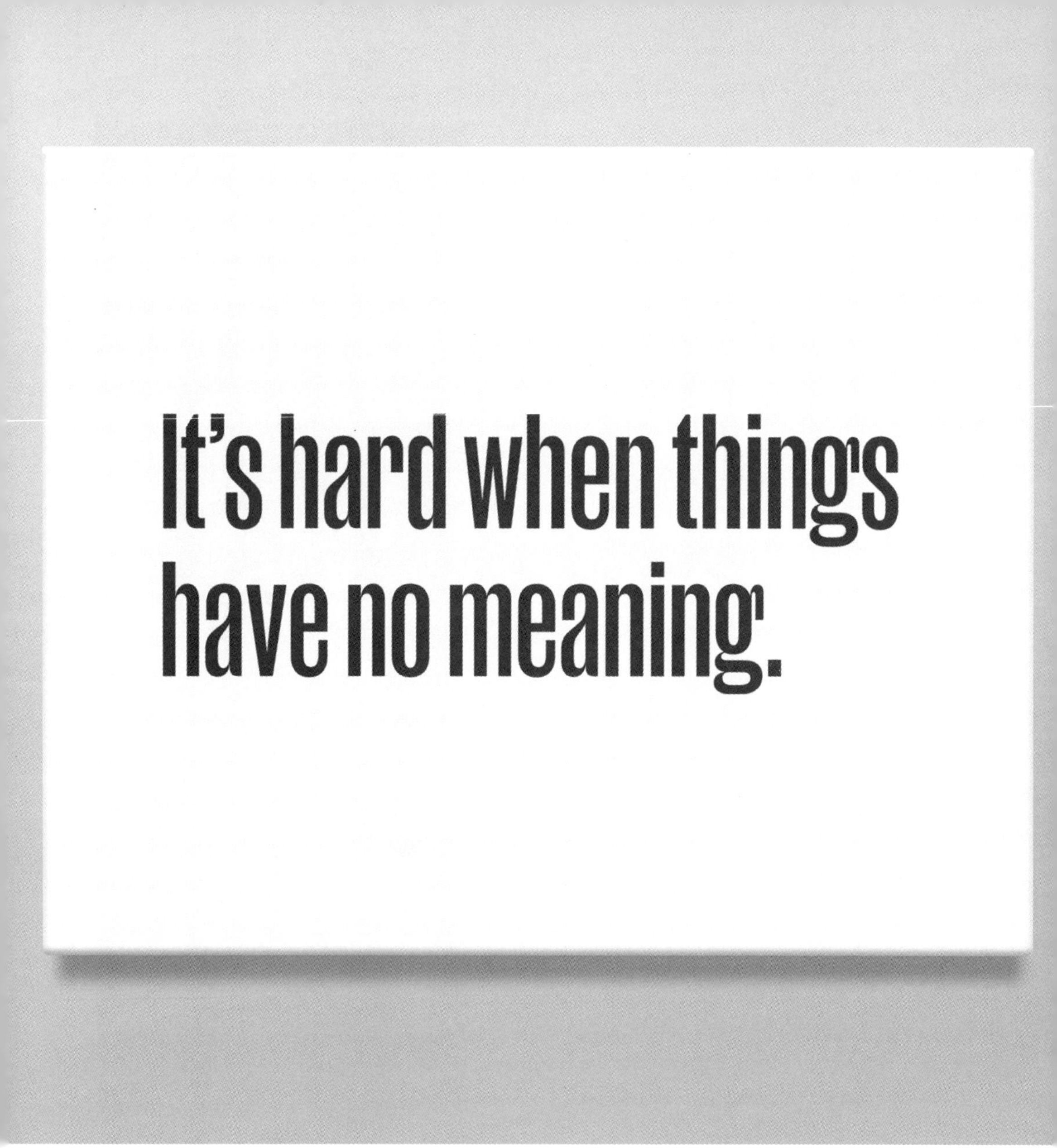

It's hard when things have no meaning.

James R. Ford, *It's Hard When Things Have No Meaning*, 2021, acrylic on canvas, 600 x 750mm.